DISCOVER YOUR
DHARMA

DISCOVER YOUR
DHARMA

A VEDIC GUIDE TO FINDING YOUR PURPOSE

SAHARA ROSE

WITH A FOREWORD BY DEEPAK CHOPRA, MD

CHRONICLE PRISM

Library of Congress Cataloging-in-Publication Data
Names: Ketabi, Sahara Rose, author.
Title: Discover your dharma : a vedic guide to living your soul's purpose /
    Sahara Rose Ketabi.
Description: 1st Edition. | San Francisco : Chronicle Prism, 2021. |
Identifiers: LCCN 2020029059 | ISBN 9781797202068 (hardback) | ISBN
    9781797202075 (ebook)
Subjects: LCSH: Self-actualization (Psychology). | Dharma.
Classification: LCC BF637.S4 .K478 2021 | DDC 158—dc23
LC record available at https://lccn.loc.gov/2020029059

Manufactured in the United States of America.

Design by Gretchen Scoble.
Typesetting by Maureen Forys, Happenstance Type-O-Rama.
Typeset in Archer, Brandon Grotesque & PF Regal Display.

10 9 8 7 6 5 4 3 2

Chronicle books and gifts are available at special quantity discounts
to corporations, professional associations, literacy programs, and other
organizations. For details and discount information, please contact
our premiums department at corporatesales@chroniclebooks.com or at
1-800-759-0190.

CHRONICLE PRISM

Chronicle Prism is an imprint of Chronicle Books LLC, 680 Second Street,
San Francisco, California 94107
www.chronicleprism.com

DEDICATION

This book is dedicated to you, for honoring the dharma that lives inside of you and allowing the whispers of your intuition to be louder than the noise of the world around you. Thank you for asking yourself the question few do and discovering the gifts you were born to share. The world is a brighter place because of you.

TABLE OF CONTENTS

FOREWORD

. . . .

harma is an ancient Sanskrit term translating to "the evolutionary impulse of the universe" or "your unique purpose in the world." According to the law of dharma, the universe is like a jigsaw puzzle. You are a piece of this puzzle, and there are no spare parts. Each of us was born with talents that play a role in serving the cosmic web of the universe, bringing about global equilibrium. The only thing holding us back from using these talents is fear, the most dangerous human construct. As Rumi once said, "I want to sing like birds sing, not worrying who listens or what they think." This is exactly what dharma is about.

In *Discover Your Dharma*, author Sahara Rose guides readers on how to find their purpose in a world where information is vast, paths are unlimited, and overwhelm is abundant. She speaks into the challenges many readers face and brings them to light with insight, understanding, and humor. Sahara has a unique ability to translate ancient wisdom in a way that is accessible and relatable to her generation while upholding its depth and significance. As you read this book, you will see that it is clear that she is embodying her dharma and masterful at laying the path for readers to step into theirs. This is the third book of hers I have had the pleasure of introducing, and I have enjoyed continuing watching her blossom over the years into the thought leader that she is today.

Discover Your Dharma is a timely book to help readers decondition their minds, remember their essence, and step into the purpose they were born to express. Today more than ever, the world is calling forth citizens to uplift humanity through the path of joy and fulfillment. This book ignites the spark that exists in all of us to share our gifts and be of service. May this book help you remember your limitless potential and live each day in alignment with your dharma.

—DEEPAK CHOPRA, MD

Why the F Am I Here?

The eternal question may have popped up after a sweaty yoga class when you were pretty sure you left your body, while watching an epic sunset that no Instagram filter could do justice to, or at an awkward holiday party where your uncle is trying to engage in a political debate. It feels like such a big question that moments after asking, we often dismiss the massive void of not knowing the answer.

We busy ourselves by playing ping-pong with the world—responding to our overflowing inboxes, never-ending to-do lists, social media feeds, and today's stressor—all distractions from the biggest eternal question. Why are we even here? This thought lingers over our actions, but very few of us actually entertain it deeply enough to find the answer. It's like getting dropped off at a random party and wondering if they have guacamole or salsa, without even wondering why you're at the party in the first place.

We spend our lives making ourselves busy and filling time, not realizing that we've been given this time for a reason. The very fact that you're at the party means you have something very important to bring, and the party won't be complete without you sharing it. More important, *you* won't be complete without sharing it.

I know you may be thinking, "Sure, I see other people having these profound purposes, but I'm not sure it applies to me." Do you think the universe happened to slip up and forget to give *only* you a purpose? If that were the case, wouldn't you be the most special person of all? You have a purpose. If you're here, there is a reason. This lifetime is about figuring out what it is.

If you don't believe me about having a purpose, I'm just going to lay it out to you and tell you your dharma right here on page 2. **Your dharma is to raise consciousness.** And so is mine. And so is your mom's, your bestie's, your partner's. We are all here to elevate the vibration of this planet we call home. However, the way each of us does it is going to be unique. We all bring different elements to the party—some of us bring the dance moves, others the snacks, others the decorations, others the rituals, others the stories, others the magic tricks. Together we create the most epic party called life.

Your dharma is the truest expression of who you are. **When you're living in alignment with your dharma, there is no separation between the outer and inner you.** Your external reality reflects your internal world. Every aspect of your life is a conscious choice. You are tapped into an endless stream of creativity, passion, and inspiration, which is the cosmos running through you. You have goals and also remain open to the mystery of the journey, trusting that your dharma will take you exactly where you need to be. You allow yourself to unfold into who you are becoming and celebrate each stage of your journey, knowing it's preparing you for the next. You feel completely alive, awakened in your senses, with an ignited flame burning in your heart. This is living your dharma.

Most of us live our lives feeling numb. We eat food, but we're still hungry. We scroll, but we're still searching. We have success, but no satisfaction. We have the information, but no clarity or embodiment. We spend our whole lives looking for something to fill this void where only dharma can reside. Your flavor may be chasing status and spin classes, or bad boys and booze, but both are distractions keeping us from the truth of who we are. This discovery is revealed only when we surrender to the path of dharma.

Living your purpose is the ultimate form of self-love. When you say yes to answering your higher calling, everything you've been seeking naturally manifests. The fulfillment, happiness, abundance, clarity, confidence, worthiness, and peace you've been yearning for effortlessly arise because you are living in harmony with your truth. There is no more striving—you simply are you, full-time. This is called embodying your dharma, your soul's purpose.

Your dharma is your divine purpose on this planet, your soul's essence, the unique vibration only you can carry out in the world.

To discover your dharma is to realize the truth of who you are. You cannot know your truth and *not* shift your life to be in alignment with your dharma. You can't unsee what the third eye saw. Once you experience it, anything else will feel suffocating.

My Personal Path to Dharma

I never set out on a mission to discover my dharma. Like most of us, I never gave it much thought. As a child, I just knew I wanted to help people in any way possible. This led to me volunteering with NGOs in many developing countries, teaching English at orphanages in Zimbabwe, advocating for human rights in factories in Vietnam, and building preschools in Nicaragua. In college, I was teaching health and sanitation in the slums of New Delhi, India, when my own health started to deteriorate. I couldn't digest food without crippling pain and stopped getting my period for two years. My bones were constantly getting injured, I had become underweight, and I was losing my hair. My body stopped producing hormones and was essentially going into perimenopause—at age twenty-one. I went to countless doctors, who each prescribed me a long list of medications to take indefinitely to live a semi-functioning life.

I knew intuitively that there had to be a deeper reason for my body's imbalance and took matters into my own hands. This journey of self-healing led me to discovering Ayurveda, the world's oldest health system and the sister science of yoga, based on the mind-body connection. When I read about the three Dosha archetypes in Ayurveda, especially the Vata Dosha (air archetype), it was like I was reading my autobiography. Every imbalance I experienced was listed. But more than that, my personality was described to a tee: creative, visionary, thinks outside the box, but also anxious and overwhelmed with thoughts. Never before had I felt so understood.

I spent the next two years studying Ayurveda in India, finding ways to merge it with modern nutritional science and plant-based recipes. It was as if I was relearning a language my soul had spoken for thousands of years. After completely reversing all of my health problems and shifting my personality to be more driven, dedicated, and grounded (which was my true nature behind the imbalances), I knew I had to make this wisdom accessible to people who suffered physical and mental imbalances like me and couldn't find a cure. Though I had never written a book or even met an author, I embarked on this journey and discovered myself in the process.

This process led me to living alone in huts in India and the jungle of Bali and writing my book while rewriting myself. I had to leave everything behind, including the approval of my family, who threatened to disown me for choosing an alternative path. It caused me to reprogram my thoughts and limiting beliefs and realize how much I had been living for external validation. I didn't know "if" I was going to make it, or even what "making it" looked like, but I knew for certain that the path I was previously on was not where I wanted to end up. There were so many times I considered just giving up, choosing a "normal" life, and making my family happy—but I knew I wouldn't be honoring my soul. I had to let go of my need for my family's approval, but more important, I had to give full approval to myself to follow this path without knowing where it would take me.

Those years were a battle between anchoring belief and quivering fear, moments of complete clarity and others of complete doubt, and feelings of total alignment and total failure, which brought me to this concept of dharma. There was a reason why my journey was so difficult—it was preparing me with the strength I needed to truly share this wisdom with the world.

Just as you may, I had a serious case of the "Who am I's" and "What ifs," and there were moments I let them drive the show. But what topped all of those fears were the "Imagines." "Imagine if I was able to get this book out into the world. Imagine the lives it would touch. Imagine the difference it would make." The Imagines ended up winning the battle. This led to me writing two books, *Idiot's Guide to Ayurveda* and *Eat Feel Fresh: A Contemporary Plant-Based Ayurvedic Cookbook,* which went on to become bestsellers. Oh, and to walking up to Deepak Chopra at a conference and to him writing the foreword (I'll share that story with you in Chapter 2). It brought me to launch the *Highest Self Podcast* because I was genuinely so hungry for deep, spiritual conversation; it quickly became the number one spirituality podcast on iTunes, currently with over sixteen million downloads. And it brought me back to this concept of dharma.

The reason we balance the mind and body is so we can regain touch with the soul. True wellness is not just perfect digestion or clear skin, but knowing the truth of who you are and shifting your life into alignment with that. The purpose of health is so you don't have to worry about health anymore and instead can bring your energy toward focusing on your dharma.

Your dreams are not an accident. The very reason you have them is that within them lies your dharma. You will never have an idea you don't have the ability to bring to life. That idea *chose* you as its ideal messenger because you are the perfect person to make it happen. However, that doesn't mean it's going to happen instantly or easily. **The obstacles you must overcome to bring that vision to reality are the training you need to *embody* your dharma and share it with the world.**

You were born with unique gifts that you're meant to share with others. These gifts may not be fully nurtured, but they are there, waiting for you to tap into them. Perhaps you are aware of these gifts but fear is stopping you from sharing them. Or perhaps your ego won't allow you to remember what they are (as your ego is just the bodyguard of your soul). Don't worry—through reading this book and following practices I teach you, you'll remember. It's not so much about *finding* your dharma as much as it's *remembering* your dharma. In this book, I'll be speaking directly to the part of you that knows.

Though my journey began with Ayurveda, the story I ended up sharing again and again was the story behind the story—how I created this reality. I genuinely believe the universe assigned me to one of the most complex, ancient, and unknown topics to show others that if I was able to make Ayurveda happen, you can make ANYTHING happen.

What I've realized is Ayurveda doesn't just inform us about our health, but on a deeper level about who we are. It teaches us to harmonize the mind and body so we can be guided by the subtleties of our souls. In this book, I'll be sharing with you how your Doshas (Ayurvedic mind-body type) are related to your dharma and how to bring your dharma through your chakras into reality.

Through my podcast, I have interviewed hundreds of people on their dharmic journey and found a common thread. Here it is:

The Dharma Discovery Journey

STAGE 1: SELF-AWARENESS
You realize there has to be more to this life than what you've been living. You know that you have a purpose but have no idea what it is. Frankly, you don't even know where to start. It feels like you've been placed in this life with no choice and simply can't go on living this way. You know you need a radical change. Through pain or numbness, you are called to take action and transform your life. This is where the seed of dharma is planted.

STAGE 2: SELF-IMPROVEMENT

You make it a mission to improve yourself. You may begin practicing yoga asanas, following inspirational people on Instagram, reading self-help books, listening to motivational speakers, using a meditation app. You've begun changing habits that are no longer serving you. This stage is focused on the physical and mental level more than the soul level. This is where the seed of dharma is watered.

STAGE 3: AWAKENING

Your interest shifts from improving yourself to knowing yourself. You begin to realize that you are not your body or your mind, but rather a soul living in a body with a mind. You are hungry to learn about every spiritual topic such as yoga, meditation, Ayurveda, ecstatic dance, shamanism, and more, which may have brought you to the Highest Self Podcast. *You may do some solo travel to spiritual destinations like Bali, India, or Peru, or have the desire to. Your entire worldview shifts as you become aware of the limiting beliefs passed down intergenerationally and begin to do the healing work. Your family and friends may not recognize you anymore and label you as crazy. This may be a difficult phase where you face loneliness, but know that you are making these important shifts to come in alignment with your truth. You begin to realize that there is a whole world of possibilities you haven't been aware of before. This is when the seed of dharma sprouts.*

STAGE 4: HIGHER CONSCIOUSNESS

You are out of the spiritual closet and no longer feel the need to hide your beliefs to be taken seriously. You have

found the practices that resonate with you and begin shar-
ing them, perhaps on social media or with your family,
friends, and colleagues. You know that you have a dharma
but you aren't exactly sure what it is and are still in the dab-
bling stages. It becomes increasingly obvious to you that
your current job is not in full alignment with who you are.
You continue your spiritual growth through shadow work,
ancestral healing, plant medicine, and/or past life regres-
sion. You no longer operate from victim consciousness and
have realized life is happening for you, rather than to you.
You have emerged as an entirely new you and people begin
asking you how you did it. This is when the dharma sprout
begins to grow.

STAGE 5: STEPPING INTO YOUR DHARMA

Through embodying who you are, you realize the deeper
purpose of why you are here. You remember your sacred
mission on this planet. Suddenly your worldview tran-
sitions from me to we. Your spiritual practice becomes
something so much greater than you; it becomes the foun-
dation from which you heal humanity. You are fueled by
the cosmos and tapped into universal life force streaming
through you. You transform any part of your life that is not
in utmost alignment because you see how it is holding you
back from your mission. You realize that you are here to
be of service and through following your highest joy, you
serve the world. You see that you are only a channel for
this cosmic wisdom coming through your vessel. This is
the space in which you truly embody your dharma and the
truth of who you are.

WHERE ARE YOU ON YOUR JOURNEY?

Most people reading this book are most likely on Stage 4—you are well on your spiritual journey, but you're missing what that dharma is. You may also be on Stage 3, and your awakening brought you here. You could be on Stage 2, and just reading this has moved you to the soul level. Or perhaps you're on Stage 1, and somehow this book ended up in your hands—congrats, you're about to speed track through your growth! No stage is hierarchal and not all of us go through these exactly, but they serve as a baseline of how many people's dharmic journeys evolve.

I do want to mention that even though you are born with a dharma, that doesn't mean it's inevitable. While your dharma is your soul gift on this planet, you also have free will. You can take that gift and stuff it in the closet, never to see the light of day. (Most choose that option—it feels easier to pretend you don't have a purpose than to confront it head on.) Or you can run with it, share it, and watch it multiply and unfold (I recommend this one). Your dharma is the gift that just keeps giving as soon as you start paying attention.

This book will tackle the most major question of life: What is my soul's purpose? But this time, we're taking a new approach, the ancient way. The wisdom of ancient times is making a comeback to guide us on the next level of our evolution. As we awaken, we remember the codes we carry in our body, which inform us of our soul's purpose for being here. As we unravel the fears, limiting beliefs, and expectations placed upon us by the outside world, we find ourselves realizing that our truth lived inside of us all along. **You first have to let go of everything you are not to step into who you truly are.**

In this book, I'll be sharing my unique approach to discovering your dharma through the Doshas and chakras. You'll discover your Dharma Archetypes and walk away knowing exactly where to focus your energy at this time with your Dharma Blueprint. I'll be offering you my personal stories, realizations, and reflections on dharma embodiment, with the purpose of illuminating your path. I don't have all the answers, but I do ask all the questions, and sometimes the answers find me. I am a channel for this sacred wisdom that comes through me from the underlying energy that connects us all.

There are many incredible books out there with more historical and mythological information on the Vedas, which this book does not cover due to its length and nature. I invite you to continue your studies of Vedic teachings, as there are lifetimes of wisdom to uncover.

Right now is the most important time to discover your dharma. We are in the midst of the greatest global awakening in human history and are being asked to step up, shine out, and turn our lights ALL the way on. Frankly, it's the only way the Earth can come back into balance. It is no coincidence you're reading this book at this time. Your soul is ready to radiate in ways you didn't even know were possible.

Hi, I'm Sahara, and it's great to meet you again in this lifetime. I promise to keep the vibes high, the wisdom deep, and the dharma strong. Let's level up the vibration of the planet, shall we?

1

Defining Dharma

W e're all on a quest to find happiness. We look for it in people, places, possessions, and all other things, but we still can't seem to find it. Where is the damn thing? I'll tell you. It's beneath its tree: purpose. Happiness is the fruit that stems from purpose. This fruit cannot grow on its own. We cannot incubate it, confine it in a lab, get only happiness without the roots, sap, and branches it comes with. We all think we want happiness, but what we really should be looking for is purpose.

We may experience moments of joy without purpose, only to go back and look for something else to take us out of our numbness or misery. True happiness comes only from fulfillment. It's when you can look at all areas of your life and wholeheartedly say, "I am living my highest truth."

The universe is benevolent and wants us to live our purpose; therefore it made living our purpose feel good . . . and not living our purpose feel like shit. You feel happiest when you are rocking your gifts because that's what is best for the whole. Happiness is our natural indicator that we're living in alignment with our purpose. It is our compass guiding us in the right way. Happiness is not the goal but the byproduct. So instead of searching for happiness, let's search for fulfillment, and happiness will meet us there.

Happiness is not your purpose. Happiness is a byproduct of living your purpose.

It's time for us to expand our understanding of what happiness is. We chase for it in fleeting moments, yet at our core, we are already bliss, *ananda*. Happiness is not a roller coaster ride or raging concert (though those things can certainly make you happy). It's the emotion that stays between these experiences, knowing that all areas of your life are in alignment with your truth.

Happiness is not about escaping but rather being present where you are. It's loving the journey, not just hustling through it for the destination. Happiness doesn't always even look like a smile on your face. Sometimes it's the fire in your heart that fuels you to change. It's the yearning inside you to create something larger than yourself and watch it come to reality, through your energy. It's choosing the challenges of your journey because they are bringing you where you are meant to go. It's going to bed each night knowing that you gave your all. It's seeing others benefit from you sharing your gifts. It's being a vessel for the universal wisdom that flows through you. The full scope of your emotions, your being, your gifts, your visions . . . that is true happiness.

Happiness Is Not	Happiness Is
Waiting for life to get good	Creating the life you desire
Escaping from reality	Changing your reality

Happiness Is Not	Happiness Is
A destination	A journey
Always a smile on your face	Sometimes the fire in your heart that fuels you to change
Avoiding challenges	Choosing the challenges that will bring you to further truth
Keeping your best ideas to yourself	Seeing others benefit from you sharing your gifts

Your journey toward embodying your dharma won't *just* make you happy. It will also make you feel fulfilled, inspired, exhilarated, as well as triggered, scared, unprepared—all of it. **Your dharma will show you the depth of your emotions, and that is the meaning of life: to experience your totality in this human experiment**. Being a human is hard, but purpose is what makes this journey worth taking. It's what keeps the busy mom going, the ill person fighting for their life, the healer helping others, the teacher showing up every day. Purpose is our life force.

As kids we always asked "Why?" "Why is the sky blue? Why do the ants march in a line?" When did we stop asking?

Somehow along the way we became too busy to ask the important questions, like "Why we are here?" and "How can we best use our time on this planet?" Instead, we've accepted our mundane reality, not knowing that within it lie the keys to our greatest awakening. The things that make us happy make us happy for a reason. **Happiness is the path of bread crumbs to your dharma**.

Each of us was born with unique gifts that only we can share with the world. Our most joyful human experience is when we can share them. When we look at life as an opportunity to show up, shine our light, and have fun along the way, life takes on a whole deeper meaning.

This is why discovering your dharma is the most important work you can do.

You may have heard the term *lightworker* (someone whose work is to bring more light to the planet), but I see us as *sun-beings*. We aren't working for anyone but are here to embody the sun that lives inside each and every one of us. When we discover our dharma, we meet our sun. When we share it, our rays expand, healing the collective shadows of the world. There is no separation between who we are and what we are here to cause and create. We live in our fullest expression, effortlessly radiating out our magnificence. This naturally awakens the sun in others too and allows them to see that the North Star they've been seeking was already inside them. Each of us rises as our own galaxy, holding hands together in the sky. Thank you for saying yes to the call of the sun-being.

WHAT IS DHARMA?

The word *dharma* is a Sanskrit term with over sixteen different meanings, but the one we'll be rolling with is "your soul's purpose." Your dharma is your big why, the reason you're here with all these thoughts, needs, and desires. We were each born with a unique purpose and this human experience is about remembering ours.

The first concept you have to understand to fully receive this book is that you are not your body or your mind, but rather your soul. You live in your body and have an operating system called your mind, but neither of them are *you*. You are the consciousness that lives within.

The second concept central to this book is reincarnation. **You've chosen to incarnate on this plane for a very specific**

reason, and that is to remember the truth of who you are. In Vedic spirituality, we are souls that exist across time and space, in multiple lifetimes. During the course of each lifetime, we learn important lessons that advance our soul. We choose to incarnate on this planet because it is the Earth school—it is the only place in the cosmos where souls can come to grow.

Before incarnation, we have each chosen soul lessons that will prepare us to embody our dharma—our soul's purpose. Your soul chose to incarnate in this body, in your circumstances, with your parents, at this point in time, because it was the exact environment your soul needed to embody its dharma. We step into the *maya*—illusion—with the purpose of remembering the truth of who we are. We agree to the temporary amnesia—being born in this human costume, forgetting the magic that we are inside. **The journey of remembering is what prepares us to embody our dharma.**

However, remembering is hard in this Earth school where fear has largely taken over. As children, we know our magic. We dream big and don't apologize for it. But the fears of our surroundings and society build up. You may have been told you were crazy, out of touch with reality, or even made afraid of your own intuitive ability. We give up our power to others who claim they know us better than we do ourselves. We no longer trust our creative impulses or speak our truths. We become a shell of the version we once were.

Think back to a time in your life when you were totally free. Maybe it was running naked outside or writing fairy tales about mystical beings or creating potions with herbs and plants. That is the truth of who you are, and she is still inside of you. All you have to do is remember.

Your dharma is encoded inside of you. Your calling is to recall who you are.

Your potential is limitless. If you knew how powerful you truly are, you'd be laughing at why you ever doubted yourself, even for one moment. You'd see that everything you wanted was wanting you back. The reason you wanted it was that it was always yours— the temporary amnesia made you forget.

Your soul has chosen this lifetime before birth because it's the experience needed to fulfill your dharma. Your soul may have chosen difficult parents or circumstances because it's exactly what you needed to gain the strength, patience, and awareness to fulfill your dharma. The healing you do in this lifetime is not just for yourself but for your entire ancestral lineage.

For example, I was born into a lineage of female suppression, child marriage, and lack of opportunity. So I came back as a fiery-ass female ready to kick the old paradigm's booty, fully embody my purpose, and remind women they are goddesses. You too are a person in your lineage who is meant to heal the ancestral wounds. It's major work, but I promise you it's 100 percent worth the ride. **Remember—you are your ancestors' greatest dream.**

I want you to take a moment and think about your ancestors.

What have they gone through?

....

....

What is the common thread that has been passed along throughout your lineage?

....

....

Are there any intergenerational traumas that have been passed down?

....

....

How are you, in this lifetime, bringing them to the surface to be healed and transmuted?

....

....

Just as we were born with ancestral baggage, we were also born with lineage gifts. These may come directly from your parents or grandparents or ancestors further back with whom you may not be familiar.

What have you learned from your maternal lineage?

....

....

What have you learned from your paternal lineage?

....

....

How are you your ancestors' living dream today?

....

....

I was gifted my mother's zest for life and my father's determination, a wonderful balance of yin and yang. My last name, Ketabi, literally means "book" in Farsi, Hindi, Arabic, and Urdu, and my ancestors were publishers. It is no coincidence that my dharma is to write books and share this wisdom with you.

You may be wondering, "Why would we be born with a temporary amnesia that made us forget our dharmas if the universe wants us to embrace them?" Because the purpose of this human experience is to go through the journey of remembering your dharma. This journey is what prepares and unlocks the power, wisdom, strength, and vulnerability you need to truly embody your dharma. **You were born knowing, but only through the quest of remembering are you ready to embody.**

We all want the same things, but not in the same ways. We all want to experience love, fulfillment, freedom, peace, and joy. However, the way each of us experiences these attributes is unique. It was meant to be unique so we can experience diversity as a species—this is the key to happiness. Source (consciousness, the universe, God/dess, whatever you like to call it) could have created every flower the same way, but it created spring cherry blossoms and summer hydrangeas and autumn sunflowers and winter roses. Each flower blossoms in its own expression, at its own time, so the entire world can relish its specific and temporary beauty.

Dharma is the same. **Just as we need the diversity of the flowers in order to appreciate them, we need the diversity of dharmas for us to appreciate them.** We were designed, like nature, to bloom at our own times and in our own ways.

We live in a world that takes one flower and idolizes it (everyone should be the red rose) to the point where we have lilies and orchids trying to dye their petals, change their fragrance, and get petal surgery to look like the red rose. We were not all meant to be red roses and thank Goddess for that—they'd get real old, real fast. Instead we get to enjoy diversity.

You were born as the unique flower you are so you can share your signature expression with the world. We need to hear the way only you can explain things, the creations only you can create, the writing only you can channel, the ideas only you can have, the support only you can offer. Otherwise, there will forever be a void that you were born to fill.

Imagine if this lifetime was a talent show, and we all showed up with the exact same song memorized and the same outfit, down to the hairstyle. We spend our entire lives preparing for this one moment—and the crowd is so bored we can't even get applause. They've heard it, well, about seven billion times. This is pretty much what we are doing right now.

We were each born to come to the talent show to perform our own soul-written songs, in our own handmade outfits, in our own crazy ways. We were born with that WOW factor. But instead, we're all trying to sing the same song. We've been conditioned to forget who we are and spend our lives trying to fit into a role we were never meant to play. It's time we show up to the talent show with the gifts we were born to share.

The world needs diversity. If everyone had the same talent, it would no longer be a talent. It would just be #basic. The facts that Tara can sing with her unique tone of voice, and Rosie can teach yoga in her unique way, and Alyson can channel with her unique guidance, and Cassandra can cook vegan recipes with her unique taste are what MAKE these things cool. Diversity is what attracts us to certain things.

When we think "But nothing about me is unique!" we just have forgotten who we are. No one here was born as a clone of someone else. You don't have to do anything to become unique—it's an inherent part of your nature.

You aren't meant to be liked. You're meant to be weird.

These words awoke me one night in a dream, coming so loud and clear. I looked up the origins of the word "weird," which was originally related to destiny, fate—essentially, dharma. Your weird-ness is your divine expression. To be weird means to be wired in your own unique way. The biggest reason so many never discover their dharmas is because they're too afraid of rocking the boat. The truth is, that's where your dharma is. You aren't meant to be liked by everyone, to get their stamp of approval and live an ordinary life. Generic is not a good look on you. You are meant to be out of the ordinary, quirky, eccentric, bizarre, magical, mystical you.

Discovering your dharma is a natural result of discovering your truth. This is why so many people make major lifestyle changes after spiritual experiences. To go back to working their unfulfilling jobs now feels like being confined in a cage when they've realized they're a jaguar. When you recognize your enormity, anything less will feel criminal. Realizing your truth can be a moment in time—however, shifting your lifestyle to be in alignment with it is where the #werk is.

DHARMA IS A LIFELONG PROCESS

Discovering your dharma is not a one-time process—it's a commitment to forever coming back into alignment. Once you know what dharma feels like, you'll instantly know what dharma does *not* feel like and can shift accordingly. You no longer get stuck in a situation that doesn't serve you—you can sense it the moment things feel off and shed the snakeskin the moment it even starts to itch.

Our life's #werk is to continually transition our external circumstances to become more in alignment with our truth. The more you see yourself within, the more your outer reality changes. At first that may be choosing to surround yourself with high vibrational people or setting boundaries with family members. Soon it may be leaving that job or moving. Throughout your life, you continue to see more of yourself, and your only job is to continue to align with it. It's that feeling of adjusting from a yoga position that feels a little awkward and learning that one tweak that makes it feel just right.

Truth is eternal, but your version of it evolves as life unfolds. Your truth today will be different from your truth a couple of years ago, given all the factors of your life. The people around you change, the society also transitions, your career's landscape shifts. Therefore, you cannot put a stake in the ground and say, "I got it; I am now in truth territory," because the ground that stake is in will move. Even if you do not change (which is impossible), the world around you will.

I share this because we often think that once someone has discovered their dharma, that's it, the work is done and life is now a disco. You can discover your dharma and then find yourself back on the path again. You are going to evolve, as will your dharma's manifestation. As long as you are anchoring back into your truth, you will always know the next step, even if it feels far away.

The universe is always tugging us in the direction of our dharma, through excitement and curiosity. We must remain open to that pull. Most of us are so busy pushing that when the universe tells us "Google that; take that workshop; learn from that person," we shut it down and say "No, I already know what I'm doing." Your job is to listen. Honor your curiosities as if they were gems given to you by the universe. They carry the information you need to get to the next step. And sometimes that next step isn't a full-blown career. Sometimes you just needed to learn something, experience something, try something.

Sometimes our dharma requires us to do something just for the love of it for years to gain the experience before we're ready to share it. Imagine if you became a chef without first learning to feed yourself. Sometimes the skill you gain from an interest helps you in other aspects of your dharma. Learning to cook teaches you patience, preparation, and thinking on your feet, which may benefit you in your career in life coaching. It's not always a direct translation from loving to cook to becoming a chef. And sometimes it's totally unrelated and just for the fun of it!

Embrace the new interests the universe sends you! You may have a weird sudden interest in all things knitting, and that may be the exact skill you need for your dharma later in life. Maybe you're creating a new sustainable department store, or making sweaters for your colleagues, or maybe you're just cultivating presence. Don't try to figure it all out—this is the working of the mind. For example, around the time of writing this book, the universe guided me to finally take action on my dream of learning how to DJ. By no means was it the "right" time—it was the busiest of my life. I had this book to write, my membership community, Rose Gold Goddesses, to launch, and was in the middle of a stressful move that wasn't going as planned, but I honored that nudge and signed up for DJ school. Whenever it was time for class, I'd think of all these reasons I was too busy, but I went anyway and came back buzzing with excitement. Today I use my DJ experience to facilitate healing and embodiment through dance workshops to bring women back home into their bodies to reconnect with their Goddess essence. During the first month of the quarantine of 2020, I showed up on Instagram Live every single day, guiding my community to dance away their fear and come back into their hearts. I received thousands of messages saying these dances helped them get out of deep dark depressions and even suicidal thoughts. Had I not followed that nudge and signed up for school, I would not have been able to literally save lives and activate a major part of my dharma: to make the spiritual journey ecstatic, fun, and playful. We are all conduits of the divine's message flowing through us. Don't block the flow. Trust your interests. They're guidance from your soul.

What are you interested in right now?

....

....

What would you love to practice but feel you don't have time for?

....

....

When will you start doing it?

....

....

Not all your interests have to turn into your career. Discovering your dharma is *not* about monetizing every one of your hobbies. In today's entrepreneurial-focused environment, we often start daydreaming about what a career as a backup dancer might look like because we went to one class. Chill. You can still do things for fun without them going on your résumé.

Your dharma is about what you want to *share*. You may *love* something but not necessarily want to *share* it with others, and that's totally OK. I love yoga but I definitely don't want to adjust sweaty people #justsaying. But if I did, then you bet I'd be at the next yoga teacher training.

Your dharma lies in the things you deeply want to share but may be afraid to. You may feel you aren't experienced enough, educated enough, old enough, young enough, etc., for anyone else to listen. We'll talk about overcoming those thoughts in this book. If the desire to share is there, it is related to your dharma.

WHY YOUR FAMILY MAY NOT BE DOWN FOR DHARMA

The concept of dharma is simultaneously ancient and new. Think about your parents: Did they live their lives according to their dharma? Did they even know what a dharma is? What about your grandparents? Did the thought of even having a life purpose cross their minds? And their parents? And theirs?

Our modern ancestors (in the past thousand or so years) most likely had no concept of dharma. It's not something taught in schools, nor is it passed down in communities. Your purpose was to get married, have kids, and make enough money to support them. Your obligation was to your family and community, not your highest self. You were taught to sacrifice, not question.

However, the concept of purpose is having a much needed comeback. We are awakening, remembering our full potential, and going back to the concepts that prevailed in ancient, more mystical times. Though our grandparents never knew about dharma, our great x100 grandparents did. We know deep in our bones that getting by is not the full human experience—we want depth, meaning, purpose. As one of the first generations in modern times to really demand a higher purpose, we are experiencing the backlash of those who grew up in the old paradigm and can't comprehend our desire for truth.

"What is this 'truth' you're seeking? The truth is that life is hard and no one likes their job, but you just have to live with it." That's what I was told. But I knew that part of me would have to die for another part of me to live. And in the battle of choosing who to kill—the me today, or the potential future me—I knew which one I wanted to live with.

Saying that you're looking for your life purpose to someone whose life was focused on survival is like complaining that your concert seats were too far away to someone who couldn't even get tickets. It evokes guilt and anger.

Many of our parents never got the opportunity to ask themselves what their purpose is; therefore, they don't understand us seeking for it. It can feel like a "first world privilege" even though it's our fundamental birthright. No one should have to live a life where they are not in control of the decisions they make. Preventing someone from living their purpose because they didn't get to live theirs is just perpetuating the damage.

We are living in a time when we are defining our own roles. Often, our family can't even understand what we're doing, let alone be supportive of it. Most of our dharmas are outside career counselors' lists of options.

Believe it or not, following your dreams is not just a myth. It's real. Your only responsibility in this life is to follow the inclinations of your soul. You don't owe this life to anyone but yourself. Not even your parents, although they birthed you. You are a sovereign being and this lifetime is yours to fully own.

After going through my health crisis and moving to India after college, I felt called to go to Bali. I booked a one-way flight, thinking I'd stay for two weeks. I ended up spending the next six months, peeling away the thoughts that were so wrapped in my consciousness, I actually believed they were mine. Thoughts like "You will never make money doing what you love"; "Only certain people get to live their purposes. The rest of us have to just get a stable job and be realistic"; and "I could never be that free and just do whatever I want; my family would kill me."

I had a burning desire to write a modernized Ayurveda book to bring this ancient healing to people who needed it like I did. I had no experience in the publishing world, nor did I know anyone who had. But this calling felt truer to me than anything I had known.

But definitely not to my parents. "When are you coming back and getting a normal job?" they'd ask me. At first I'd play it off, like this was just a temporary thing and after this Bali stint I'd come back and be a "normal" human. But the more I ecstatic danced and breath-worked, the more I realized that this *is* my truth. My spirituality is not meant to sit on the sidelines. It is who I am.

This unlocked generations of ancestral guilt that lived inside of me. Like many children, I was living for my parents' approval. But moving to Bali and India to write a book on Ayurveda without a book deal or business plan? That was something they wouldn't get behind.

The conversation between us got tenser as time went on. "We sacrificed everything for you to grow up in America and have opportunities we never had. We gave you everything, and this is how you repay us? This is the most SELFISH thing you can do, just going to Bali without thinking about how your parents will feel. You HAVE to come back. Enough of these childish games. Time to get back to reality!"

Even though I was in one of the most beautiful places in the world, these were some of the most difficult times of my life. I danced between anger and sadness, guilt and confidence, blame and forgiveness, trying to understand whether living my own path was indeed selfish, crazy, and wrong, or whether "selfish" is another word incorrectly defined by society to make us feel wrong about choosing ourselves.

It would have been easier to believe in myself had I known I'd "make it." But I had no evidence. Maybe my parents were right to say that trying to become an author is like trying to become a starving artist, that I'd end up homeless, selling pants on the beach. (Well, I actually did that and it wasn't so bad.) Maybe I was delusional, out-of-touch with reality, a wishful dreamer who would one day regret taking a risk and not treading the safer path when I could? Maybe one day I'd look back and laugh that for some reason I thought I was special? I'd ask everyone I met, "Do your parents know you're here? What do they think about what you're doing?" Some would tell me their parents were there with them; others that they hadn't spoken in twenty years.

The tension with my family got worse. Threats were made to send me to a mental asylum because I told them I meditated under a waterfall with a shaman and saw the negative energy being released in the water, turning it a dusty gray. The more I'd open myself up to my parents, the more they'd shut me down with their own fear and resistance. I was the catalyst of "ruining their lives" by choosing to live my own. I realized I couldn't yoga this tension away. Eventually I had to come back to the United States to speak to them face-to-face, at this point strong enough in my own truth that their fears weren't enough to trigger my own.

Returning to Boston, to my childhood home, felt like being in a weird museum full of things you used to know but that feel nothing like you now. My flesh may have been the same, but my soul felt entirely different. By societal standards, I had nothing—no job, no security, no stability. But on the inside, I had met a part of myself that I didn't even know existed, and I wasn't going to let her go.

"One day, I'm going to be a spiritual author like Deepak Chopra, but helping young women in my generation," I told them.

"You are delusional. You are out of your mind. Who do you think you are? You aren't a doctor. You aren't an expert. If you want to open your mouth and help people, you better get your PhD. This is what happens when hippies influence you!" was their response.

I remember our most traumatic fight to date. At the time, it felt like an attack on my being, but today, from a higher perspective, I can see that it was out of love. My father's way of protecting me was to stop me from doing what he believed was a mistake or an infringement on my safety. The only difference was this time it wasn't his child running after a ball on the street but rather seeking to live life on her own terms. In yet another confrontational "So what are you going to do with your life?" conversation, tension arose when I declared I would never get a normal job. In helpless anger, my father yelled that I was a "loser and failure" and that I "was not his daughter," as he'd never raise a daughter so careless.

Those words stung me, as the one person I tried to impress my entire childhood essentially proclaimed me dead to him. I see now that he was trying to protect me from a life of "uncertainty" and was willing to do anything he could, even if it hurt me, to snap me out of it. However, at the moment, all I felt was deep, deep pain that ached in my heart. I ran down to my childhood room, the only place I could be alone, slammed the door, and fell to the floor weeping. *Was this all a lie? Do they tell you to follow your dreams as a kid but then you grow up and just assume that it was all bullshit? Was I still believing in a Santa Claus that didn't exist?* I wailed on the floor, my tears creating puddles on the ground, my stuffed animals staring at me with sympathy.

And then I felt the void. I felt nothing, and in that I felt everything. I realized I was already a failure in their eyes. My greatest fear had been actualized. I was essentially dead to them. Therefore, I didn't have to live for their approval. I only had to live for my own. This was the moment I became free.

Suddenly, I felt a lightness within. I am a sovereign-ass being! It actually doesn't matter what they say or think because I don't have to listen to it! I don't have to explain my choices to anyone! If they don't want me in their life, then great! Because *I* want me, the real me, all of *me,* in my life. And that's when I became *unfuckwithable.*

I went out to nature and shamanic shaked, releasing all stagnant energy from my body, as the neighbors watched me and my parents shook their heads in disapproval, still thinking about how I belonged in the psych ward.

Several days later, I declared, "I'm going back to India," this time without any hesitation or question in my voice. "I'm going to be leading a retreat in Goa, sharing about the Goddess wisdom with my friend from Bali."

"Seriously, you're starting with this nonsense again?" my dad responded.

"Yup. Leaving next week."

The energy was different, as if they could sense this newfound anchoring that wouldn't budge regardless of what they said. Their words went through me and I knew at my core I was going where I was meant to be.

And off to India I went for the next several months, this time being fully present without second-guessing whether I was actually "supposed" to be there.

I had to break the child-parent bond that made me think I still needed my family's stamp of approval before I proceeded. When I freed myself from that bondage, I truly dove into my soul assignment. I stopped wasting time thinking *if* I could do my dharma and began actually *doing* my dharma.

You won't figure out your dharma by sitting on the sidelines, dipping your toe in, waiting for the perfect opportunity. You have to take the leap, and that requires taking off the seat belt that's holding you back. I switched my focus to writing rather than explaining. I wrote an entire book called *Eat Right for Your Mind-Body Type*, worked as a health coach, paid to get my book completely edited and designed, and figured out how the publishing process worked.

Was it an instant success? No. I got rejected by thirty publishers who echoed the same fears I used to have: that I was too young/inexperienced, that no one cared, that I wasn't a doctor, that Ayurveda was never going to happen. But I knew, deep in my soul, that this book was meant to be on the shelves of Barnes & Noble.

Through a series of synchronicities, the literary agent who pitched my failed *Eat Right for Your Mind-Body Type* book was asked by another publisher if she knew any Ayurveda experts to write the official *Idiot's Guide to Ayurveda*. They had an author who was four months into their six-month deadline and quit because it was too much work. They needed someone to write a four-hundred-page textbook on Ayurveda, start to finish. She suggested me and they responded with, "I don't know, she seems young [I was twenty-four at the time], but have her write a sample table of contents and first chapter and we'll give it a read."

That day, I went to Barnes & Noble and read every *Idiot's Guide* book I could find. I stayed up all night writing that table of contents and first chapter. Two days later, I was hired. The two years I spent writing *Eat Right for Your Mind-Body Type* had prepared me to produce this book. I worked on it diligently for two months, writing sixteen hours a day as the wisdom channeled through me. It wasn't *the* modern Ayurveda book I wanted to write, but I knew it was a foot in the door. After that I learned everything I could about book launches, pitched myself to podcasts, and made that book a bestseller. As soon as it was published, I finally got the chance to write *my* modernized Ayurveda book, which I called *Eat Feel Fresh* (named after the blog I began at nineteen that started this whole journey).

I didn't have a plan—but I kept following my excitement and moving forward. You don't need to see the end of the highway to start driving. You just have to keep taking action and let the universe meet you halfway.

I wouldn't give up those years for anything because they are what made me strong and capable. Looking back, I know that Source created that situation *for* me because it gave me the courage I needed to do the work I do today. I had to break up with the parts of myself that still lived for external validation, replacing them with my own validation. I had to believe in myself because I didn't have the belief of those whose opinions I valued most. Finding the courage to be me even when I wasn't supported by my parents gave me the strength to bring this work to other people who may be riddled with the same doubts. Discovering your dharma isn't about always knowing where you are going, but rather about following what feels true for you at this time. This clears the way for your dharma to come through.

Through the journey of embodying my truth, I realized that many of us struggle with discovering our dharmas because we don't believe we are worthy of them. The generation before us struggled, and we've taken on their fears. We're living life thinking

"How can I survive?" instead of "How can I thrive?" What we must realize is that our current reality is very different from theirs and it is fully safe to be us. Because of their hard work and sacrifice, we are blessed to not have to worry about survival, and for that we must be eternally grateful. Today even older generations are remembering that they too have a dharma. It's never too late as much as it's never too early.

I see a comparison to the psychologist Abraham Maslow's hierarchy of needs. Only when you've had your survival needs met can you contemplate luxuries like finding your true purpose. But what happens to people who grow up comfortable? They desire more. They don't see the purpose of devoting their life to a paycheck because they can see the discontent and stress it brought their parents.

If you feel like you owe your parents a stable job to keep them happy, realize you don't owe your parents your future—you owe that to yourself. Your parents will have to come to terms with the fact that you are a sovereign being. Honestly, that's a cosmic lesson they've signed up for, and it's not your right to keep them from it. Don't hold back your progress for the fear of disapproval, because then you just disapprove of yourself (and that's the person you'll always have to live with). There are a lot of lessons for both parties involved. (By the way, you're never going to be the loving child you think you are by holding yourself back from your dharma, because if you do that you'll always resent your parents.) Who knows, you might even encourage them to discover their dharmas too.

The generations before us didn't see others finding success in their passions, but rather in following established professions. If they drew a little bit outside the lines, they were putting their careers at risk. Today, the ones who excel are those who draw outside the lines in vibrant colors. We live in a new world that's constantly evolving, and it's up to us if we want to hop aboard the train or grab onto the former paradigm that no longer holds.

Though our parents may not have grown up with the opportunity to discover and actualize their dharma, this doesn't mean it is selfish of us to. Each generation progresses, and we mustn't limit ourselves to the opportunities available to our parents and grandparents. They did their best with what they had. Today we have access to a lot more, and our children will have even more than that.

In today's world, the internet has allowed us to share information faster than ever. Now it's possible to work remotely from anywhere in the world, start your own brand, share your message, and co-create with others. We're seeing our friends and acquaintances chase their dreams, and it inspires us to follow ours. All the information we could ever need is there—what we need now is the embodiment.

When you embody your truth, you inspire others to embody theirs. Flash forward six years, and my parents are my biggest fans. They share my books with everyone they meet and display my magazine covers. Not only are they proud of my work, but they have begun their own. They know their Doshas, have ecstatic danced, and they've been to my workshops and retreats. All the tensions between us have dissipated, and we are able to love each other more than ever because the relationship is based upon mutual respect. I wouldn't have the relationship with them I have today if it hadn't been for the transformation it had to undergo. Sharing this story publicly for the first time is the final release of the old wounds from those years, alchemizing them so they can heal others. When we own our stories, we are no longer bound by them, and we realize the power we have to write our own.

A QUICK RUNDOWN
FOR YOU SKIMMERS

You were born with a dharma because you were meant to share it. You were meant to share it because we need you. We need you because the world has problems. The world has problems because people are not living their dharmas. People are not living their dharmas because they've forgotten. They've forgotten because they're afraid of being weird and making other people uncomfortable. However, today we are waking up to the understanding that it's a myth that life was meant to be ordinary, and instead we're remembering who we are and how we were meant to share our expression.

All of this may sound new to you, but trust me, it's not. Your soul knows what's up, and the fact that you are reading this is activating your cellular memory. You may come back to this page a few months from now with an entirely new understanding. It may feel over your head, but it's already in your heart. When you stop thinking and analyzing, and start trusting and listening, it will all make sense. Don't stress it. It's all happening anyway. All you have to do is follow the excitement, sun-being.

2

Kriya + Karma:
Guiding the Way to Dharma

Picture it this way: You were born on a highway. At the end of the highway is your dharma. It's like those signs leading you to Disney World that start three states away. You know it's coming and you're so excited, but you're just not there yet.

As you're cruising down this highway toward your dharma, you're tempted by a lot of different exits. One exit says, "Come over here and be a stock trader. You'll make lots of money!" Another says, "Head this way to become a doctor and make your parents happy!" Another says, "You're not going to be pretty forever—become a model and make the most of your good looks while you still have them!"

It's easy to get off course. I mean, who knows, maybe they're right? Maybe this Dharma Land doesn't really exist, and it's all just a bunch of hocus-pocus you're told as a kid. Only celebrities get to follow their dreams, not normal people.

You see your friends getting off the highway to take those exits. They seem so confident! Andy the astronaut is becoming Andy the accountant! Ilia the inventor is becoming Ilia the IT manager! Hilary the horse trainer is becoming Hilary the HR assistant! They aren't ecstatic about it, but hey, there are benefits. And it's safe.

So you're tempted. You start veering left when suddenly you feel a bump. Then you feel your car swerve out of control for a couple of seconds. Then you hear this voice saying: "What are you doing? You were meant to be a healer!"

You turn up the radio louder and keep heading toward the next exit, until suddenly you crash into the highway barrier and total your car. You're totally shaken up. It feels like something greater than you took the steering wheel. That's because it did.

This is karma. When most of us hear the word *karma* we think of the Justin Timberlake song "What Goes Around . . . Comes Around." While that is one interpretation, karma also means "action," and in this definition, karma is bounded action by the universe to keep you in alignment with your dharma.

Karma is the highway barrier. When you choose not to listen, it reminds you of your destination with a light nudge, and then a tap, and then a punch, and then eventually a collision. It will speak louder and louder until you listen. It's a warning sign, out of love, because the universe is trying to support you. Karma isn't out to get you—it's protecting you so you stay in alignment with your truth.

Now imagine you're driving on a Sunday, on cruise control, with no cars ahead of you, down that Dharma Land highway. You're bumpin' to your favorite music and nothing's in your way. You pick up momentum and before you know it, you're taking pics with Minnie Mouse at Dharma Land. This feeling is called *kriya*, or flow, a boundless action to spring you toward your dharma.

Doors just seem to be opening up for you, and one thing leads you to the next. You're meeting the right people at the right time, encountering the right opportunities. It almost feels like you're taking a passenger seat in your own life, totally trusting that the universe is bringing you exactly where you need to go. You're cruising, baby.

Believe it or not, this is the way we are supposed to live. But for some reason, we've collectively agreed to the false story that life is meant to be a series of unfortunate events just because so many generations have been living in karma. When something good happens we brace ourselves, because something bad must surely be on its way.

But we aren't supposed to feel stagnant, stuck, and half alive in this human experience. Kriya is supposed to be our normal—karma is a sign something is off. When you are in alignment with your dharma, the universe propels you in the direction of your dharma in ways you never could have yourself. And that's how life was meant to be lived.

Kriya in Action

Since I was twelve, I've been reading Deepak Chopra books, and they have guided me on this path. In 2017, I was at a Yoga and Science Conference in New York City, and I thought to myself, "Imagine if Deepak Chopra walks onstage." As we were called to lunch, the announcer said, "And a hello from our sponsor, Deepak Chopra!" He walked onstage, waving quickly to the crowd as they began to leave the room. I was shook. I knew that this was probably my only chance to see him in person, and I needed to thank him for his work. Something larger took over me and guided my body through the crowd of a thousand people leaving the auditorium and onto the stage where he stood. He looked at me and something along the lines of these words came out of my mouth: "Hello, Dr. Chopra, I'm a huge fan of your work and it's been so influential in my path. I recently wrote my book *Idiot's Guide to Ayurveda*, which is really going to help bring Ayurveda to millennials, and I'd love to share it with you." I had no expectations—the book was going to be released in a few days. I was just grateful to meet my hero.

The next day I was on my way to a meeting when I heard a man say, "Can someone help me cross the street?" I turned around to see a short man with discolored skin helpless on the sidewalk. A voice came to me: "Sahara, if you think you're such a good person, help this man." I was halfway across the street, running late while simultaneously eating (not very Ayurvedic of me), but something came over me. I walked over to him and said, "I'll help you, sir; where are you going?"

"Two blocks down, to the subway, please." I detached myself from getting to my meeting in time and took him by the arm as we strolled down the busy street, talking about his life. Turns out he was a refugee from the Iraq War, and we chatted about his kids. I walked him down the subway stairs and led him onto a waiting train. Just before the door shut, I asked him, "By the way, sir, where are you going?" He answered, "University. I'm a professor of physics."

I thought to myself, "Wow, I never would've imagined that." I was feeling pleased with my "Humans of New York" experience when I checked my phone and saw an email from Deepak Chopra, asking to call me. I freaked. On the phone, he asked me to meet him at his lecture on Monday in San Diego—and I was flying back to LA the next day, so the timing worked perfectly. After the lecture, he said he was impressed by the book, generously offered to write the foreword, and asked me to join his faculty. I was mind blown, out of body, pinching myself. Suddenly, my life had drastically changed from striving so hard to make my book happen to Deepak Chopra writing the freaking foreword!

In that moment, I realized that the old man hadn't been a man at all but an angel. It was Source testing me: Would I respect a person as much if they were not a famous author or helping me in any way, but were keeping me from my agenda? The fact that I said yes is what caused all this to happen. And it is no coincidence that both he and Deepak Chopra are doctors and physicists.

After all this happened, Deepak did a Facebook Live video on meaningful synchronicities, mentioning my name. (Holy crap! Is life real?) I had to send him an email.

"Hey Dr. Chopra, I recently watched your video on meaningful synchronicities and absolutely loved it, but I have a question. Is life *always* meant to be lived in flow? Or are periods of transformation meant to be followed by periods of inertia to balance each other out?" Send. Freak out that I just emailed Deepak Chopra, casually.

He responded: "Sahara, if life is not always in flow, then something is wrong."

Boom. Mic drop. Game changer.

Kriya is the new normal.

The story that I had been carrying, that good things can't last for too long, is exactly *why* they hadn't been lasting for too long. The universe was responding, "OK then, I guess I'll give you some of those problems you spend all your time thinking about!" **Our thoughts create our reality.**

What if we changed that story to: "Things are going really great right now and more good things are to come! Thank you, universe, for always providing so generously!" With those thoughts, miracles become our ordinary experiences of life and stagnation is actually the rare occurrence. Even when something difficult shows up at our front door, we know it is just a cosmic lesson that is further propelling us on our journey.

So I've been rolling with that story ever since. Life is meant to be lived in kriya, in that state of divine flow. And the moment you feel that you're drifting off path (which is going to happen to all of us, no matter how many hours of meditation we log), you can recognize it and come back into alignment toward your dharma.

When you feel yourself shift from kriya to karma, use these mantras to refocus your thoughts:

- Thank you, universe, for that rough day to remind me of my boundaries! I receive more ease to come.

- Thank you, universe, for that tough situation to encourage me to speak my truth early on! I now speak clearly and efficiently.

- Thank you for that divine reflection allowing me to see parts of myself I hadn't before. I walk the path with knowledge and courage.

- Thank you for showing me my limits. I acknowledge and honor them moving forward.

It's all just lessons on lessons on lessons on lessons. And the best part is, it's all bringing you toward your highest self.

Your Dharma Is Not Just Your Career

It's so much deeper than that. Your job is a drop of water and dharma is the ocean. It's not a title, and you can't add it to your

LinkedIn page or résumé. It's about tapping into your frequency, the one only you can emit. Your dharma is the role you play in this life that combines all of your strengths, your passion, and your aptitude into one.

Imagine your dharma as your mission statement and your career as an offering you provide. For example, your dharma may be to serve and protect victims of social injustice. That may manifest as a lawyer, activist, documentary maker, nonprofit founder, or a host of different careers. Your most aligned career will reflect your dharma, but your dharma is much more than that.

We live in a culture where burnout, stress, and hating your job are the norm. All this means is we are not living in alignment with our dharma. Burnout only happens when you are not listening to your truth. When you are, you are tapped into limitless energy, creativity, and inspiration.

When you discover your dharma, all that is not in alignment will change, and that may include your career. Imagine learning the very reason why you came on this planet, then spending most of your life doing something that has nothing to do with it. Following your path to dharma may not mean an instant career shift, but the way that you show up in the world will undeniably evolve.

Your dharma may start off as a hobby, then naturally transition to become the thing that supports you. For example, you may love helping people with their relationship issues, and years later realize you'd like to become a relationship coach. Making it your career is taking it to the next level. The goal, however, isn't to find your perfect job. It's to find your truth and realize your only purpose is to express that.

Many of us feel guilty about charging for something that we love, and there is often an expectation that any healing service should be free. This limiting belief is holding so many back from living their dharmas and truly bringing the world that healing it needs. Would you tell a doctor he shouldn't charge because he is supposed to help people out of the goodness of his heart? Would you tell an artist to give you her painting for free because she enjoyed painting it? Then why would we expect something else from any other type of healer? (PS: Exposure doesn't pay your rent.) Loving your dharma and using it to heal others should be the norm. As we awaken, we must honor and recognize the time, effort, love, and dedication that went into any dharma and see it as valuable.

We all need financial abundance to survive and thrive in today's society. Your time and dedication to your craft require energy and therefore an energetic return. For you to take your dharma to the next level, you must be comfortable charging. Not only will people value your energy more, but it will allow you to use your time more effectively to focus only on your dharma. Not charging is not helping anyone unless you genuinely feel called to, or are offering it for underprivileged communities who cannot afford your rates.

It's not just *what* you do but the energy around *how* you are doing it that makes it your dharma. People often fear there is no more "room" for them to do their dharma when they see others on a similar mission. Imagine if a writer said, "Oh man, someone else is already a writer, there's no room in the market for me." Just because there is another self-love coach doesn't mean they can work with everyone who needs more self-love. One person cannot solve all of the world's problems; each person can serve a unique demographic of people that best connect to them.

Two people could express the same thought, but the way they say it and the energy around it can be totally different. A teacher may say, "It's important to meditate to improve memory," while an activist may say, "We must all meditate for world peace." They're both advocating the same thing, but their motivations are totally different. That's why dharma isn't *what* you do but *why* and *how* you do it. We'll get into the Dharma Archetypes in Chapter 6.

Different stages of your life may activate different archetypes that exist within you, which you embody until they no longer serve you. For example, having a child can activate the nurturer role, but after they reach a certain age you may no longer be leading from that archetype. Your dharma is your cosmic expression—with it, you can do a million different things. How you manifest your dharma is your free will. Your dharma is always to be the unique manifestation of who you are and who only you can be.

This is why it's so important not to compare ourselves to others and say, "Oh, well. My dharma has already been taken." It has not. *No one* can do what you were meant to do in the way that only you can do it. There are a million yoga teachers in the world, but each one practices differently. There are a million actors in the world, but each stands out in their own way. We can give the exact same speech or sing the same song or play the same role, but it's always going to come across differently.

Many of us instantly jump into looking at the careers we see on social media and deciding which one is our dharma. News flash: None of them. There is no one else out there living your dharma because there is no one else out there that is you. There may be someone who inspires you, but the unique energetic signature you bring to it will have a different frequency.

Embodying your dharma is not about being liked by everyone. We aren't meant to resonate with everyone because we cannot serve everyone. Instead, we must focus on who we *do* resonate with, and serve them to the fullest.

We have to speak our language so our people can find us. If the words I've written so far have been resonating with you, then you're my people. If you love ancient wisdom as much as you love 2000s hip-hop, then you're my people. If you love to chant mantras and sometimes drop an F bomb, then you're my people. If you're appalled and ready to ask for your refund, you're not my people. And that's totally cool, too. (I hope you get your refund.)

When we try to speak so that our mother-in-law's friends will take us seriously, we end up sounding like a Hallmark commercial. You have to be yourself, and sometimes that can be polarizing. You'll turn people off, but do you know who you'll turn hella on? Your people.

YOU WERE BORN A G. AND BY G I MEAN GURU.

In the womb, you knew what's up. You were still aware of all your past lives, gifts, and superpowers. Then you were born and forgot (part of the contract, kid). The secret of this life is that you have to remember who you already are.

You already know your dharma in your soul, but you've picked up some layers of fear, judgment, insecurity, and doubt along the way that have made you forget. It's like a lion that grew up in captivity, yet its biology still knows how to roar, hunt, and survive in the wild. Just like Simba before Nala came back.

And so we go out seeking the answers that already exist inside of us. The reason you're on this quest to know your dharma is that your soul is trying to awaken you. No career coach, guru, therapist, or teacher knows the answer to your dharma. All they can do is pose questions to help you remember.

It's in the process of remembering, of gathering experience, that you *become*. You were born with your dharma—but your experiences on the journey to find and fulfill it are what prepare you to embody it.

As children, we are more tapped into who we truly are than we are as adults. We feel no fear or hesitation around being our most authentic selves: We sing, we play, we create, we question, we learn. At a certain point, though, we're told that learning is a process of memorizing specific information that has no interest or relevance to us. We're taught that to be successful, we must fill our minds with dates and random facts and long division, none of which have any significance to our dharma.

This puts a stop to our natural learning process, stifling our progress. We realize that to make it in life, we must sit still and be quiet so that we can get a gold star from the teacher. We give away our power like we give away our curiosities, and trade the love of learning for the fear of failing. This is why school is called an institution. It is teaching us to be robots, to obey the needs of the corporate world. It was designed to create workers, not leaders. The history of the education system shows us that our public schools were based on industrial revolutionary needs to have people working long hours in underpaid factory jobs without questioning or making demands. This isn't education, and to be honest, the mainstream school system is a major reason so many of us don't know our dharmas. To succeed in school, you have to cut yourself off from a big part of your intuition and creativity, which is where the magic happens.

The good news is that you can get it back with active de-conditioning. I'm a product of the public school system, as well, and have been able to reconnect with the intuitive wisdom that runs through me. I will be sharing how you too can undertake the process of deprogramming and reconnecting in this book.

First we must unlearn the falsehoods we've learned. This can be effing scary but totally liberating. We've been passed from our parents to our teachers to our professors to our bosses, always looking to someone else for approval and direction. We're so used to the authority figure telling us what to do next, when they're only following what was told to them. We are conditioned to live by the rules, but who made up these rules? People acting from a place of fear. **This is about reclaiming the direction that exists only inside of you.**

So get comfortable with not knowing what you're doing! Discovering your dharma is like jumping into a free fall where you don't know whether a feather bed or a slab of cement is at the bottom, but you're trusting it's the former. If you're confused, you're on track! Confusion opens up the space for possibilities. It's a much more heightened state than apathy, or certainty about a destination that isn't in alignment. It's better to *not* know where you're going than to know you're going in the wrong direction. I used to be labeled as "confused" for trying so many new things, until I flipped that word around. I wasn't confused—I was curious. **When you transmute confusion to curiosity, you open up a realm of possibility.** You are testing out new potentials in the discovery of your truth.

Most people are so afraid of temporarily not knowing that they never truly know. They'd rather stick with the familiarity of their safe jobs than entertain the idea that there can be something more out there. That potential feels way too overwhelming, so they'd rather pretend that it doesn't exist. However, at a certain level of consciousness, it will become so uncomfortable and so suffocating to remain in your limiting waters that you'll have no choice but to break free. By surrendering to the unknown, you create the space for finally, truly understanding.

The only way we can know is to *not* know. We want a twelve-step process to living a life of ultimate happiness, abundance, purpose, love, sex, and flat abs, all for the affordable price of $99.99! That's not the way that dharma works. No one can guarantee you'll make it because no one knows your destination. You only figure that out through the process.

Each step of the way is the building block to the next one—and there are no cheat codes. Your experiences shape you for the opportunity. We want to "make it" when "making it" is a result of the process it takes to get there. **The journey toward your dharma is your unique training to embody your dharma.**

Living your dharma is a path less traveled because it requires courage and commitment. However, at a certain level of consciousness, you can't *not* want it. It lingers in your mind and becomes louder and louder until you say yes.

We can distract ourselves with the busyness of life, but life without dharma is food without salt. Even when our dharma means less time having "fun," it brings us a greater sense of joy than any beach day or brunch could. It's the real-deal fun. This doesn't mean that you no longer want to do things outside of your dharma, but they become less of a priority. They're the things you do to fuel you up, so that you have more energy to give to your dharma, not the other way around.

Sometimes the hardest part is distancing yourself from your dharma and living your normal life because you're passionate about what you do. When you're glued to your laptop because you're so in flow, that's how you know you're in your dharma.

Dharma feels better than any drug, any dance, any date. It can make you want to lose sleep and dedicate all your free time to it.

> If you're counting the minutes until it's over,
>> it's not your dharma.
> If you haven't even realized hours have gone by,
>> it's your dharma.
> If there's something else you'd rather be doing,
>> it's not your dharma.
> If you prioritize it over all other things,
>> it's your dharma.

Having a dharma is like having a baby. They cry, scream, puke, poop, and keep us up all night. They're not always easy, fun, or joyful. A lot of times they can be a freakin' burden. But you love your kid more than anything. You're willing to stay up all night with them, spend every waking minute with them, and make them the center of your world. That's how your dharma will feel. Your baby's smile is the equivalent of your dharma's growth. Each milestone fills you with so much joy that all the struggle is worth it. It makes you realize that what you've created is so much bigger than who you are.

When Your Lower
Brain Is Talkin' Shit

Our brain is composed of two parts—our lower "survival" brain and our higher "universal" brain. Our lower brain is our reptilian brain, the part that has helped us survive up until this point. It's always on the lookout for what could potentially go wrong in any situation. It's the part of your brain that makes you stress out about a work email for your entire vacation. It focuses on any perceived difficulties that it believes could threaten your survival. That's why we humans pick a cloud from a clear blue sky and dwell on it until we've created a thunderstorm. Our lower brain's job is to keep us safe. According to your lower brain, sameness = safety. Therefore, it will favor situations that keep you exactly where you are.

Your higher brain (the prefrontal cortex) is focused on unity, joy, expression, and bliss. It is the part of your brain that already knows your dharma—but it's subtler than your lower brain, so it's more difficult to hear its whispers. Most of us use only 5 percent of our higher brain's potential. The lower brain has shut off most of our access, causing us to act based on survival rather than dharma.

The higher brain sees the big picture. It knows that if you follow your highest path, you will not only be safe, but also fulfilled. It knows you were put on this Earth for a purpose, and that everything is divinely connected.

Listening to your higher brain takes trust. Meditation, yoga, dance, sound baths, and breathwork are all practices you can utilize to enhance the functioning of your higher brain. The more you can think with your higher brain, the clearer everything will be.

For example, do you ever go to sleep stressed out about a situation that happened in your day, only to wake up the next morning with no negative emotions around it? The situation didn't change—your mindset did. When you sleep, you clear away all conditioning and let the mind revert to its baseline, which is one of love and compassion. This is why we wake up each morning with a clean slate, on which we can choose either to paint today's masterpiece or to pollute with thoughts of yesterday.

Most of us think about purpose from the lower brain state, focusing on "what ifs" instead of the possibilities. Your lower brain focuses on "What if I never make it" instead of "Imagine if I did." Your lower brain would rather you survive in your routine, monotonous job, and lifestyle—even if it's not serving your highest calling—because it can guarantee safety. If your lower brain had its way, you'd stay in your childhood room being fed by your parents for the rest of your life. The desire to have a guarantee is our human desire to control, which actually limits what is possible for us. It is giving up our power to co-create our destiny with the universe. Your dharma is not a hiking trail that thousands follow. It requires going off trail into the jungle, on a path that you are carving every step of the way.

The higher brain's whispers are what encourage us to shake out of our cocoons and morph into butterflies, even through discomfort and uncertainty. Your higher brain knows what's on the other side—freedom, expression, purpose—but your lower brain wants the road map, testimonials, a 100 percent money-back guarantee, and travel insurance before making the journey.

The more you're open to the unknown, the easier it will be to find your dharma. This is because your dharma has yet to be created—it is defined by your journey.

Your dharma is a sunset that is forever morphing and shifting to include new colors and expressions. At any given moment it's perfection, only to be followed by another form of perfection.

Just as a sunset is ever-evolving in its rainbow of colors, so is your dharma, each moment in time its own divine beauty. We've grown up in a society that wants to prepare us for everything, but dharma cannot be prepared for. You may not discover your dharma immediately, but it will plant seeds in your mind that will later sprout into dharma pods, once you water them with thoughts and action.

THE PATH TO DHARMA

What are you drawn to?

What does that say about your energy?

What were you drawn to in your childhood?

What did that say about you?

How have the things you've been drawn to changed?

WHAT'S YOUR VIBE?

As you rise in consciousness, you naturally radiate that energy to the people around you. I call this the vibrational domino effect. When you're in a high-vibration state, your energy and actions create a natural ripple effect on others. And when you're in a low-vibration state, you also emit that energy to others. Let me give you two scenarios.

Scenario 1

You wake up in the morning, meditate, make tea, and go to work. Your colleague forgot to send something to you on time but instead of freaking out, you smile and say, "Don't worry about it. Just give it to me when you have a chance."

Your colleague goes back to their desk feeling relieved and grateful for your compassion. In their high-vibration state, they decide to invite the new girl in the office out to lunch. She's so overjoyed that someone reached out to her that she goes home and tells her boyfriend how kind everyone at the office is.

The boyfriend, who had been worried whether his girlfriend would like her new job, feels relieved, and it removes a lot of the tension he was carrying. When he calls his mother that night, he speaks with compassion and love. His mother feels so heard by her son that it instantly brightens her day and helps bring her into healing. She lives a longer and more joyful life, all because you didn't snap at your colleague. Profound, right?

Scenario 2

You wake up in the morning, frantic that you slept through your alarm, run out of the house disheveled, and stop at the coffee shop. You're getting agitated while waiting in the long line and the barista can feel your energy as you rattle off your order without even looking up from your phone.

The barista feels unseen, unheard, and overwhelmed, and ends up messing up your order, which leads you to cause a scene. This creates more tension in the already chaotic coffee shop, which sets everyone on edge. Each person leaves feeling more stressed out than before, carrying that energy to their respective offices.

You snap at your colleague that the work should have been done the day before. The new girl doesn't get invited out to lunch. She goes home crying. Her boyfriend is brusque with his mom on the phone, which causes her health to further deteriorate and lifespan to decrease. And that domino effect repeats in office after office all across the city.

Now, these are two very different outcomes, both of which you had some level of responsibility in, however distant. We are always responsible for the vibration we carry. A positive vibration state will create more unicorns, rainbows, joy, and laughter. A negative vibration state will move like smog, making everyone more sad, lonely, and hollow.

At any moment, you choose your vibration. Which are you going to roll with?

ARE YOU AND YOUR DHARMA A VIBRATIONAL MATCH?

You want to know your dharma badly; I can feel it. But are you a vibrational match for it? You tell me. Imagine your dharma is that person on social media you so wish you could be real-life friends with. If they came over and you complained about how annoyed with life you are the whole time, how nothing ever works out for you, how you must be the dumbest person on the planet because your life sucks the most, are they going to want to stay for dinner? We want to be around high-vibe people—and that starts with being a high-vibe person. Your dharma is the same way. It isn't going to hang around while you recount everything that's gone wrong that day. It'll show up when you show up.

You are only going to fulfill your dharma to the extent that you are a vibrational match for it. Even if you *know* your dharma, you're not able to *embody* it unless you can remain in a vibrational state high enough to *fulfill* it. Simply put, you can't do your best work when you're feeling like shit. You have to take care of your vibrational state first, so your dharma can flow through effortlessly.

We're all human radios picking up on unseen energies. This is how you can just *feel* if something is off or that a person's true intentions may not be clear—you are using your vibratory senses. Have you ever felt that a friend is having a bad day simply by the way they're texting you? Or have you ever met someone and felt an instant soul connection? Have you ever walked into a room and felt like something just went down there? Or walked into a home and either felt the love or that something is off? These are all examples of how we pick up on subtle vibrations every day.

We're all born high vibrational—look at the prana (life force) of a baby, so pure and full of life. However, somewhere along the way, we lose that natural-born innocence. We focus on the negative because the world around us does.

Your life is a reflection of your vibration. When your vibes are high, you are unstoppable. You are a manifesting machine. You say something and it shows up on your doorstep in a bow tie.

You may say, "You know, I'd really love to connect with Alyson," and next thing you know, she's texting you. Your life is a web of synchronicities, each taking you further along the path toward your dharma. This is living in kriya, and this is your birthright.

When you're in a low-vibrational state, the opposite is true. One thing leads to the next and your vibe keeps getting worse. The thoughts in your head are spiraling downward, as are the situations in your life. This is the power of vibration. We are all making daily choices that affect our vibration. It may be something we are doing only for a minute, like gossiping, rushing, or worrying— but even one minute can have a lasting impact on our day.

Taking care of your vibrational state is key to finding your dharma because you're never going to embody it when you're down in the dumps. Sure, life will throw obstacles at you that may bring down your vibration temporarily, but it is your opportunity to learn how to bring it back up. **When you transmute your obstacles into medicine, you create alchemy.** You must find the tools that work for you to take you from a low vibe to a high vibe. It may be a dance party in your living room, a kundalini practice, a walk outside, or a meditation. Just one simple act of self-love is all you need to turn that vibe upside down, and from there, you're all the way up!

Your vibration is your choice. Negative things might have happened to you, but they do not define you. Experiencing hardships does not destine you for low-vibrational tendencies—indeed, those who experience hardship often recognize the importance of positive thinking and have the highest vibrations. Some of the highest-vibrational people have had extremely challenging lives, and some of the lowest vibrational people have had everything handed to them.

We always have the power to bring up our vibration. It can be as easy as giving a genuine compliment to someone, texting a friend about how much we appreciate them, teaching something we know to someone, wearing an outfit that makes us feel cute, helping a person who is struggling, decluttering our work space, volunteering our time, spending a weekend in nature. These little decisions make a big difference in our overall vibration, which allows us to manifest our dharma.

Your dharma will require you to reach a level of alignment that you most likely have never reached before. Your dharma requires all of you. You'll have to show up in ways you never have before and tap into sides of you that you didn't know existed. Obstacles will come your way, but remaining in a high vibrational state will allow you to transmute them into lessons on your path. The good news is that once you've enhanced your vibration, you'll know exactly how it feels when you're off and how to increase it again when you're out of balance.

The life you experience is a reflection of your internal reality. There is no "out there"—it's all in here. The Vedas are the first-ever recorded texts channeled by *rishis*, spiritual sages in northern India, on how we can live our optimal human experiences. They are the basis of yoga, Ayurveda, meditation, astrology, chakras, and many other forms of holistic sciences we practice today. These texts run in my bloodline and I feel I am embodying my ancestors, who originated in these very lands, when I channel this text to you. The Vedas say, "As is the microcosm, so is the macrocosm." It's the difference between choosing to start your day with affirmations and a morning routine, or anxiety and stress. These little decisions create your larger vibration, which creates your entire world.

So what are you attracting? Are you meeting the right people at the right time? Are you finding the exact books, podcasts, and teachers your soul needs to hear? Are you channeling ideas and stepping into the flow state? This means you're living in kriya, effortless flow, and in a high vibrational state.

Or does life feel like you're putting out one fire after the next? Shitty things just keep happening to you and you don't even know why—and honestly, it makes you feel sorry for yourself. You don't know what you need to focus on and keep procrastinating because you already have so much to do and feel like life's not fair. This is living in karma—and all these negative emotions are a reminder for you not to continue walking this path and turn instead toward your truth. From one good thought comes another. So just start with one little reminder, one little dance move, one little moment of self-care. Each of these acts of self-love guides us to the next and before we know it, we vibin' high.

Remember—we are always manifesting, not just when we're writing down our goals. The vibration you put out there is the energy that will come back to you—and we always have the opportunity to raise it up.

WAYS TO RAISE YOUR VIBRATION

- Meditate (see my Discover Your Dharma meditation in Chapter 4).

- Try my Dharma Embodiment Practice (Chapter 8).

- Practice affirmations such as "I am in alignment with my dharma" (more in Chapter 8).

- Practice tapping for your dharma (learn how in Chapter 8).

- Sing loudly and unapologetically to 2000s pop music.

- Play some music and let that booty bounce.

- Write a list of what you're grateful for.

- Spend time with a pet or a loved one.

- Call or meet with a friend and talk about what's going great in your lives—no complaining allowed.

- Have a Dharma Circle (I teach you how in Chapter 9).

- Walk in nature.

- Read a book or listen to an audiobook/podcast.

- Stare at the stars or ocean.

- Let the sun hit your skin.

- Watch your favorite Disney movie.

High vibes are the road map to our dharma. When you're living your dharma, you feel energetic, uplifted, like you could do this forever. Time passes and you don't know where it went. You leave an activity feeling more energized than when you started. It's like the cosmos just drip IV-ed you some fairy dust and you're on one.

What are the things that make you feel *more* energized afterward? For me it's speaking onstage, dancing, and recording podcasts.

What are the things you do that make you feel like time just flies? Maybe it's being deep in conversation or thrift shopping or researching sustainability.

What makes you just feel GOOD? Maybe it's when people tell you how funny you are, or when you have a day to yourself to just write, or when someone said you transformed their life, or when you're playing music.

Vibes don't lie. Follow what amps them up.

A QUICK RUNDOWN
FOR YOU SKIMMERS

You were born on the dharma highway. When you're cruising, you experience kriya, boundless action by the universe, aka that flow life. When you get distracted and get off course, you experience karma, bounded action by the universe, aka get your shit together, girl. The universe is just trying to keep you on track.

So don't listen to your lower brain when it's saying you can't live your best life. That's your ego self just trying to keep you safe, aka BOR-ing. Your highest self knows what's up. Honor her, trust her, listen to her, even when it doesn't make sense and she's trying to get you on that crazy train. I know you want that 100 percent money-back guarantee, but you know that doesn't exist. Just keep raisin' your vibes and following the excitement, and your dharma will manifest before your eyes.

3

The Four Types of Dharma

We were all born with gifts. For some of us, they're obvious. That's because our society celebrates certain gifts, like singing and shooting hoops, while others, like raising a child, are ignored. Because of this, if we aren't harmonizing like Mariah or hitting three pointers, we feel like we have no purpose. Your gift may be hosting events, helping people heal through trauma, organizing homes, or inspiring people to become healthier. These gifts may seem more subtle, but they're just as profound and we need all of them.

Through my research on dharma, I've realized that although we all have a different dharma, there are various types. Some people are born knowing their dharmas, while some had to forget only to remember again. Some dharmas are developed through overcoming obstacles, while others are unveiled as the solution to a problem that's plaguing yourself or others. Some dharmas work as a combination of all of them. Let's explore what they are.

1. YOU KNOW YOUR GIFT

You know those people who just came out of the womb doin' their dharmas and nothin' ever stopped them? This is the first type. They have an undeniable gift that they came to this Earth to share. Most artists and athletes fall into this category—they were given an incredible voice or the ability to shoot a goal or tell a joke, all skills we celebrate in our society. However, that doesn't mean they're set for life. The gift was given to them, but it's up to them to determine what they want to do with it. They still must fine-tune it with practice. There's no denying that Adele was born with the gift of a powerful voice, but there are thousands of others with wonderful voices who didn't improve their skills, commit to their path, and of course have her same dharma. Some of the best musicians aren't even playing, not because they're less talented but because they did not chase their dharma the way others did. (Think of it like the joke about the man who prays to God every day to win the lottery. Finally, an exasperated God says, "Meet me halfway and buy a lottery ticket for once!")

2. YOU HAVE A BREAKDOWN AND SHARE IT

"I was on my knees, wondering if God does exist, when suddenly a voice came over me and I knew what I came here to do." These breakdown/breakthrough stories are often what you hear from coaches, motivational speakers, and authors, all of whom fall under the Teacher archetype I discuss in Chapter 6. A breakdown can be anything from a health crisis to poverty to heartbreak to addiction. From this point, you take radical responsibility for your life and transform your worldview, with a newfound sense of purpose to share your realizations with others. Your pain becomes your purpose and your mess becomes your message. These difficult moments give life meaning and allow you to heal others, and ourselves, in the process of sharing. (This is my type of dharma!)

3. YOU HAD A NEED AND ARE NOW SOLVING IT

We often find our dharmas by serving our own needs and then finding that others need the exact same thing. It doesn't have to be anything traumatic, but something we genuinely needed help with ourselves, such as support in the early stages of our business, organic baby wipes, or deliverable Ayurvedic soups. For example, author Vanessa van Edwards dealt with social anxiety and an inability to read social cues. So she studied them, even making flash cards of people's facial expressions to review. This led to her creating her blog on being less socially awkward, which eventually led to her book *Captivate*. If you have an issue, chances are someone else does, too, and they'd love to know your approach to solving it!

4. PEOPLE AROUND YOU NEEDED SOMETHING AND YOU FOUND THE SOLUTION

This is the less-talked-about way to find your dharma, but it's just as important. You don't personally have to go through an issue in order for it to be your dharma. What problem can you solve for others? You might be passionate about health because you helped your father reverse his diabetes and want to help others do the same. You don't have to personally have gone through the issue to want to be part of the solution. As we enter the new paradigm, we no longer have to experience breakdowns to find our medicine. Hopefully our children can begin their paths as healers and helpers without that firsthand experience.

You still have a dharma, even without a "life-defining" moment. There are many people who feel that because nothing "significant" has happened to them, they don't have a unique story or perspective. Overcoming normalcy can sometimes feel more difficult than overcoming a life-shattering event because there isn't that great need to shift: You can just easily float on by living a regular life without asking yourself the great big question of why you're here. However, even if you can't name one "life-defining" moment, there are many moments that have defined your life . . . and dharma.

We've all overcome something. After all, not all traumas are experienced in the same way. Divorce can cause some kids great pain and anguish that takes them years to overcome. For others, it may not be that big a deal, and they understand innately that Mommy and Daddy want to separate and that it's better for everyone. There is no comparison between unique traumas. In the end, drowning in two feet of water is no different than drowning in twenty. We often compare traumas and think that the person with the craziest life story wins, but we've all overcome some obstacles. You don't need to have a major trauma to have dharma. You were meant to share in other ways.

We're all here to raise consciousness, but in different dimensions. As a planet, we are making the shift between the third and fifth dimensions.

The third dimension (3D) is the current reality for most of the population. It's based on duality, right or wrong, fear, individualism, and survival of the fittest. Life in 3D feels like a series of random, and often unfortunate, events that you have no control over. You experience little glimmers of beauty that feel fleeting and stem from the external world. You identify with your thoughts, which often loop in negative emotions. You may have hobbies but don't consider them part of your purpose. Stage 1 of the Dharma Discovery Journey is in the 3D.

The fourth dimension (4D) is the bridge to 5D. It's still anchored in the 3D world but aware of the 5D. Awakening into the 4D realm is often triggered by a "dark night of the soul" such as a crisis, career change, or breakup that triggers dormant emotions to surface and be brought into the light with awareness. This is where we do our "shadow work." You become aware of your suppressed traumas, triggers, and fears and commit to the path of healing on a mind, body, and spirit level. You work on overcoming mental blockages that are preventing you from harnessing your full intuition. You realize the power of your thoughts to create your reality and that you were born with a sacred soul mission to share. Stages 2 to 4 of the Dharma Discovery Journey are in the 4D.

The 5D is where we are all headed—higher consciousness. In this dimension, there are no coincidences, only synchronicities. We trust the unknown, follow our intuition, and are pure embodiments of our dharma. We experience universal oneness, limitless possibility, ecstatic joy, and love and compassion for Earth and all beings. We don't give into the collective paradigm of fear and realize that we have complete control over our emotions, thoughts, and beliefs. We create our reality and live in complete unity with our truth. Stage 5 of the Dharma Discovery Journey is in the 5D.

3D: Why is this happening *to* me? (Victim consciousness)

4D: How is this happening *for* me? (Learner consciousness)

5D: How is this happening *through* me? (Creatrix consciousness)

Some of us choose to focus on the 3D, within existing structures such as the legal, governmental, or medical system. Some choose to work in the 4D, helping others with anxiety, stress, or worthiness. Others choose to work in the 5D with spirituality, energy healing, shamanism, channeling, and the unseen realm. All are important work that brings balance to the world around us. We need the friendly person at the courthouse, the woke dentist, the conscious therapist, and of course, the collective healers. Moving to 5D consciousness does not mean you'll be doing only 5D work. We are called to different dimensions to assist in the awakening. I always say we should have a foot in the 3D and a foot in the 5D to be aware of present-day "reality" and also be the bridge to the shift forward.

Which dimension do you feel like you are on?

....

....

What dimension are you called to work in?

....

....

Note: If you are called to work in the 3D world, it's ultra-imperative for you to have your practices to bring you back up to the 5D. We need you embodying your full radiance, and it's all too easy to let the fears of the world dim us down. Dancing, shamanic shaking, meditating, breathwork, yoga, painting, oracle cards, and rituals are all wonderful practices to bring you back to your 5D self.

WHICH PATH TO DHARMA RELATES TO YOU?

Do you have a natural-born gift? What is it?

....

....

Did you have one as a child that you haven't used in a while?

....

....

What obstacles have you overcome?

....

....

Have you ever experienced a breakdown moment? How did you break through it?

....

....

What are some needs you once had that you were able to meet? How did you meet them?

....

....

What do you love to help others with?

....

....

What do people ask for your support with?

....

....

Can You Have Multiple Purposes?

We all have multiple purposes and roles we play in our lives; for some of us, that manifests in different careers, and for others, it's different hobbies. There are people like Picasso who dedicate their life to their art, and people who shapeshift through different lifetimes over the course of this one. Some find their purpose early in life, like Greta Thunberg working to save the environment at fifteen, and others find it later, like Julia Child, who wrote her first cookbook at fifty. There is no one path greater than the other.

Those with more Vata (air energy) prefer to have multiple projects going on at the same time. They feel restricted by doing only one thing day in and day out and find their energy works best when they can express different sides of themselves. These are people who are bodyworkers/comedians/psychics/hairstylists at the same time. I call them "slashies." It's just how their energy works, and they do best when they aren't tied to one career. However, their dharma is the eternal strand that connects it all.

Those with more Pitta (fire energy) are all-or-nothing about their dharmas. When they find that thing they love, they go all-in. They live and breathe their dharmas, working around the clock, daydreaming about ways to build at all hours of the day. It's an extension of who they are. (This is me!)

Those with more Kapha (earth energy) find their dharmas through love. They might realize their dharma in parenting, friendships, or relationships. Their dharma isn't one goal, but rather the way they connect with the world around them. It may feel difficult to pinpoint what their dharma is because they aren't as explorative as Vatas or as determined as Pittas, but they truly feel alive when they are relating to others, and this leads them to their purpose.

You can learn more about your Dosha and how it's related to your dharma in Chapter 5.

Your dharma is eternal, but the way that it manifests may change throughout the course of your life. Let's say your dharma is to bring beauty to this world—you can do that by being a makeup artist, then a graphic designer, then a store owner. Your dharma may be to connect with people on a deep level—you may be a therapist, then a coach, then a retreat facilitator. Your dharma may be to reconnect people with their bodies—you may be a masseuse, then a yoga teacher, then an acupuncturist. The dharma is the same, but its manifestation is different.

We are always evolving, and your dharma requires you only to be the most recent edition of who you are. It's not giving up if it's honoring your truth. **Giving up is quitting something you love because of external feedback. Evolving is choosing something else because your energy has moved.** You can be an artist, healer, visionary, entrepreneur, and activist at the same time—different archetypes will just show up in different situations and your dharma is to find the unique ebb and flow between the various sides of you (more on archetypes in Chapter 6).

No one is one-dimensional. As we rise in consciousness, we realize that we all have many interests. Gone are the days when the blacksmith was just the blacksmith and the carpenter was just the carpenter. We are able to wear different hats and exercise different parts of ourselves. **Our dharma is who we are between them all.** It's the way that we show up in all circumstances and the lessons we've learned from each of them.

FINDING SPACE FOR YOUR DHARMA

Various types of dharmas and the stages they're in require different amounts of energy and attention. For example, if you're launching a new business, your dharma will require almost all parts of you. If you're still in the exploratory stages of finding your dharma, you can balance it with other areas of your life. Even when you're well on your journey, there will be ebbs and flows to the requirements of your dharma. There are seasons in my life when I'm focused solely on writing a new book and need to keep my creative channel open (Vata), others when I'm focused on speaking tours and launching new offerings (Pitta), and others when I'm resting and recharging (Kapha). I've found that keeping these time periods separate allows me to use the type of energy needed for it, whether it's more introspective writing or extroverted speaking.

There are plenty of ways you can create space and time to commit to your dharma. Many people are choosing the path of digital nomading, moving to a country where living costs are much lower so they can focus their energy on their dharma (this is what I did in India and Bali!). Even parents are opting to "world school" their children by taking them traveling with them. By cutting down on living costs, you can open up space to do things out of sheer curiosity. It is easier to play, make mistakes, and figure out your path.

You can also downsize your home and belongings, selling what you no longer need, and use that extra money as a cushion to support you on your dharmic journey. Minimalism is the move! If you have the option to move in with a family member, it can remove the financial pressure (and is totally normal in most of the world). I moved in with my grandparents when coming back from India, and it allowed me the freedom to focus on my book (and they were super appreciative of the extra help)!

While discovering your dharma, it's crucial to drop the idea of how you think life "should" be. It's OK not to have everything figured out after college, your thirtieth birthday, or a twenty-year career. It's OK to start over. Everything has been a part of your journey and has prepared you for what is to come. Sometimes the only way we can know what we *do* want is to first experience what we *don't*.

Instead of kicking yourself that it's too late, think about how much your life experiences have taught you. The career in HR could've taught you the people skills you need to become a coach; those years in marketing could've prepared you to launch your own brand; those grueling months as a server could've taught you the hustle needed as an entrepreneur. **There are no mistakes, only lessons**. See each experience as a part of the life curriculum you had to undergo to fulfill your dharma. Each job, obstacle, and difficult circumstance was another class you needed to pass to prepare yourself for what awaits.

Remember that nothing happens to you by accident. It happens to you because it's exactly what you needed to learn to get to the next edition of who you're meant to become. The harder it's been, the more rigorous your education. Now it's time to apply those lessons into your life's work, sun-being.

LET'S EXAMINE YOUR UNIQUE LIFE LESSONS BY FILLING IN THE BLANKS:

I spent time working at a ....
It taught me ....

Examples:

I spent time working at a nonprofit. It taught me how to build
relationships.

I spent time working at a restaurant. It taught me patience,
hard work, and human connection.

I spent time working at a bar. It taught me how to move fast,
work efficiently, and start conversations with anyone.

I spent time working in a lab. It taught me discipline and
organization.

I spent time working at a law office. It taught me structure and
dealing with a high-pressure environment.

I spent time working at a hospital. It taught me to deal with
loss and find joy in the little things.

I couldn't have learned .... **had I not** ....

Examples:

I couldn't have learned to stand on my own two feet had I not
been cut off by my family.

I couldn't have learned the importance of a healthy diet had I
not become sick.

I couldn't have learned the value of self-care had I not burned out.

I couldn't have learned the benefits of meditation had I not
become depressed.

I couldn't have learned social skills had I not had social anxiety.

Because I _____, **I became** _____.

Examples:

Because I suffered panic attacks, I became in tune with my emotions.

Because I was born into poverty, I became hardworking and grateful.

Because I lost a parent early in life, I became aware that life is short and we should spend each moment doing what we love.

Because I dealt with cancer, I became resilient.

Because I was weak, I became strong.

Because I felt powerless, I became a leader to empower others.

Discovering your dharma can be like walking through a dark room. When you've finally made it across the room to turn on the lights, you'll realize you were home all along. It only felt unfamiliar because you didn't know where you were. Your dharma is your home base. It's being your absolute self, a self that you may not have met yet because you've been so conditioned not to see her. Your dharma is your north node in astrology, the part of you that feels unfamiliar but is you at your very core. **At first it may feel like striving, but actually the energy is embodying.** It's no longer trying to be anyone else other than who you are.

A QUICK RUNDOWN
FOR YOU SKIMMERS

Just because you're not performing on a stage doesn't mean you don't have a dharma, too! There are four types: You got a gift (that Super Bowl half-time-show life); you had a breakdown/breakthrough (that TED Talk circuit); you had a need and now you are meeting it (that *Shark Tank* hustle); or people around you needed a solution and you found it (that Nobel Prize game). You can have multiple dharmas (we all do), and they'll reflect in the different Doshas.

Don't waste any time freaking out about not knowing yours. Drop the idea of how your life is supposed to look at this age and realize you're exactly where you need to be, learning from those soul lessons and upgrading. You only feel like you're walking through a dark room, but you don't realize you're already home, boo!

4

Doing Your Dharma

There seems to be a battle between being and doing. We commonly hear phrases like "We are human beings, not human doings" and "I'm so bad at being." While I absolutely agree that we need to spend more time being as a collective, it's not *why* we are here. If we were here to simply be, we would've been born as crocodiles, hangin' around all day and eventually eating a snack. There is a beautiful place where doing and being merge together, and that is embodying your dharma.

We are here to create. This burning desire is in us for a *reason*. This belief that it's "unspiritual" to "do" is a misinterpretation. The Vedas share that you have your spiritual practice *so that* you can fulfill your dharma. It's not about overcoming the human experience, but fully immersing yourself in the experience. **There is nothing more spiritual than to truly be here, in your body, on this Earth, living out your purpose.** It's time we stop guilting ourselves about doing and start doing what matters—our dharma. This is what I call "sacred doing."

Sacred doing is when your action brings you closer to your truth. You were born with dreams, desires, and interests because they're meant to guide you on the journey. It's not about overcoming them; it's about embracing them—they are your driving forces forward.

Our only goal as humans is to create. This is the core difference between us and animals. We were given decision-making brains, opposable thumbs, and passionate hearts because we were meant to use them. The innate desire for humans to create is what has led us to find medicine in our plants, meaning in the stars, myths from our experiences, and purpose in our years. We meditate, slow down, and go inward so we come back into clarity and act in accordance. The being is just preparing us for our sacred doing, which brings us further into our being. This is the divine cycle of life.

When you are fully in alignment with your sacred doing, you are being. There is no separation between the two. The writer becomes the words, the dancer becomes the dance, and the singer becomes the song. There is no longer any distinction—the practitioner and the practice merge.

When you go so deep into your doing, you are being. And when you go so deep into your being, you cannot help but do. Dharma is the intersection.

Most of us correlate "doing" with doing the things we don't want to do, which is why we have this war on "doing." We focus on how we can meditate or do practices to calm ourselves down, without addressing why we are stressed in the first place. What we get to ask ourselves is the bigger question—how can I create a life that I don't need an escape from, that doesn't bring up my blood pressure or put me on the brink of a panic attack? The meditations and journal prompts are what give you clarity on what you now get to do.

Dharma is the integration between doing and being, when your daily actions are your meditation. There is no separation between you and what you are doing—you merge as one, becoming whole.

Your Path to Dharma

Your dharma is supposed to be *fun*. If you were assigned to this soul mission, wouldn't the universe want you to enjoy it? It purposely made it fun for you so that you keep doing it! If you hated doing your dharma, you wouldn't do it, and the world's problems wouldn't be solved. This is why if everyone just did what they loved, the world would come into balance.

The path to dharma is the path of following joy.

There may be parts that will be a challenge, of course, but you still enjoy the process of moving through it. The challenge is worth the reward. That's how you know you're in alignment with your dharma. Discovering your dharma is an ongoing practice of taking action and learning from the feedback. Sometimes to learn what you want, you first have to figure out what you don't want. Most of us stay stagnant, not taking action on anything because we aren't sure if it's the "right" thing. The universe responds in corrective action. This is the karma I was speaking about. As you act, you receive the feedback of what feels expansive and what feels contractive. What this means is you can't eff this shit up because even if you take the wrong action, you'll be corrected through feedback. All you have to do is listen and keep pivoting toward what feels true.

THREE WAYS TO GET TO YOUR DHARMA

You may be wondering how the heaven anyone even *finds* their dharma with all of the possibilities out there. With social media, we see people becoming manifestation experts and professional priestesses and we wonder how we'll even find our dharma with so many options. I used to feel the same. Having now interviewed hundreds of guests who have discovered and rocked their dharma on my podcast, *Highest Self*, I've found that there are three underlying story arcs behind everyone who's found their dharma. Though their stories may sound different, they really are the same journey. Knowing about the ways others have reached their dharmas will open up your consciousness to finding yours.

1. The Leap

The first and most known way of finding your dharma is "the leap." The leap is exactly what it sounds like: letting go of your former comfortable life to take a leap of faith into a new way of being. This could mean quitting your job, investing all of your money into your new business, moving to a new country, or anything else that seems extreme but feels absolutely necessary to living your dharma.

Now, these are the most celebrated (and often feared) ways of discovering your dharma, but they're not the only ways. We applaud those who quit their corporate job to launch their own nonprofit . . . once they're successful. But when someone is in the midst of taking the leap, people often try to persuade them to stay on the beaten path. This is why the leap is so intense: There's so much risk, but also so much reward.

The leap isn't for everyone, but it's a guaranteed way to find yourself because you essentially *have* to make it work. You are so committed to embodying your dharma that you'll move miles, whereas if you were in a position of safety, you may only have moved inches. Everything's on the line and that makes you jump over many perceived limitations.

When you want to move but are comfortable in your current home, for example, you might scroll through Zillow once a week and check out any new listings without any real sense of urgency. Your attention isn't focused on moving, and the process is slower. However, if you moved out of your house and were in temporary housing until you found your new place, you bet you'd find that new place. You're gonna *live* on Zillow; you'll know street names like the back of your hand. You are all-in and supercharged. And chances are you'll find a new place quickly, because the uncertainty of temporary housing is pushing you to move faster and more efficiently than you would have otherwise.

Taking "the leap" works the same way. If you quit your job, you're going to figure out a way to make your business work, since your other options are homelessness or crawling back to your old job. You'll get more creative than ever before because it's your life on the line. You may take an odd job or an unpaid internship, which may not feel glamorous but provides the time and experiences you couldn't have gotten elsewhere. It's always progress if it brings you closer to your dharma.

Take my husband: He left his successful job as a real estate broker to pursue his passion of becoming a film producer. However, as the 2008 financial crisis hit, he lost his life savings in a slew of bad investments. Instead of going back to selling real estate, he knew he needed to continue his creative pursuit and became an assistant to a photographer who ended up not paying him but giving him his camera. He used that camera to freelance and began shooting for country music musicians. He learned everything he could about music management and used that experience to pitch managing a successful artist as well as doing all her photography as a perk. She said yes to that offer, and that led to starting his own music management company, where he now manages over thirty internationally touring, Grammy Award–winning and platinum-selling artists. The most mind-blowing thing? His original childhood passion, which he would have never considered as a career until then, was music.

A leap doesn't guarantee that you'll end up where you think you want to go. But I promise you, you *will* end up where you belong. You're showing the universe that you're certain the path you were on wasn't bringing you into your highest alignment, and that you're committed to embodying your dharma—whatever that means. It's removing yourself from a toxic situation and opening yourself up to what the universe has in store for you. It's exhilarating, scary, and exciting all at the same time.

"The leap" is right for you if you're an all-or-nothing person, or if the pain of staying with your job is just unbearable. If you're certain what your dharma is and already experienced in it but just need the time to commit to it, taking the leap would be a great option. If you already have revenue streams from your dharma but are afraid of stepping into it full time, I encourage you to take the leap and go for it!

Pros:

- Most transformational— guaranteed you will transform from the inside out by taking the leap.
- When you do fulfill your dharma, it is *extremely* gratifying.
- You can immediately stop your soul-sucking job and dive into what's next.

Cons:

- It can be intense, traumatic, and risky.
- If anyone is dependent on you, it can cause issues in your family.
- There will be a great deal of stress.

2. The Transition

"The transition" is the most common and safe way to reach your dharma. You may be used to the term *side hustle*, referring to that extra thing you do for additional income, but in this sense it is that extra thing you do for a purpose because it is guiding you to embodying your dharma fully. It may look like keeping a nine-to-five job that may not be fulfilling but also is not distressing, while you spend your mornings or nights researching, dabbling, or doing activities related to your dharma such as taking classes, launching a business, or building an audience.

The transition requires commitment and self-motivation because, let's be real: You're going to be tired, drained, and full of excuses after work and on the weekends. It's easy to choose Netflix and brunch over spending time on your computer trying to take your dharma off the ground in isolation, especially when you aren't getting an immediate return. However, it's completely possible and just takes prioritization. If you can come to your dharma with excitement and motivation, you'll most definitely get it off the ground without the intensity of the leap. Start with the eighty-twenty rule—spend 80 percent of your time at your job and 20 percent with your dharma and grow from there.

My friend Krista Williams worked a nine-to-five when she and her friend decided to begin a lifestyle podcast. They'd record episodes in their closet, and after several months finally got the courage to launch it publicly. They had no expectations of where it would take them—they were just following the excitement. Eventually the podcast began to grow, as did sponsorship opportunities. After two years, Krista was making enough income from the podcast to quit her full-time job. With that extra time and energy, she now plans tours across the country to connect with listeners.

"The transition" is a safe and secure way to move into living your dharma without quitting your job and potentially taking on odd jobs and the stress of not knowing how you'll pay your bills. It also gives you the benefit of time. Krista and her partner had the chance to build their audience and find sponsors before depending on their project to support them. Krista says her drive and dedication to *Almost 30*, working every afternoon and weekend for just as long as she spent on her nine-to-five, is what made the podcast so successful.

"The transition" is right for you if you aren't quite sure what your dharma is—you can try out a variety of classes, programs, and opportunities before leaving your job. (Gotta love the internet for that!) If your dharma requires a technical skill, take lessons and practice until you feel skilled enough to take the leap. If your job is bearable and still gives you the time and energy to focus on your dharma, this would be a really great option. If you are working on your side hustle but it isn't yet providing you income and you don't have any savings or are not willing to downsize, choose the transition.

Pros:
- Less risky and stressful than "the leap."
- You can quit your job when your dharma financially supports you.
- You have the luxury of time.

Cons:
- Less sense of urgency, which can make you less dedicated.
- Requires the most commitment because the pressure isn't there.
- You have to make the time even when you're exhausted.

3. The Accidental Discovery

"The accidental discovery" is when you stumble upon your dharma—it finds *you* rather than the other way around. You're just out there living your life and *boom*, your dharma hits you on the head.

My friend's uncle had been an engineer for more than thirty years when his office required everyone to take up an extracurricular activity. He "randomly" chose pottery. His first time on that wheel, feeling the fluid earth moving through his fingertips, he was hooked. He spent every opportunity he could on that wheel and is now a professional potter, which is quite rare in today's world. Part one of his life was about making machines, and part two was about making bowls. Had he not ended up in that accidental pottery class, he never would have embodied his dharma.

There are no coincidences, only circumstances that appear coincidental. The universe has far greater knowledge of our capabilities than we will ever understand. All we have to do is follow the excitement. It's like how many people in their second marriages say that their first marriage was preparing them to be the spouse they can be today. Our dharma works in the same way. We are constantly being prepared for what is to come next. All we have to do is listen and follow the excitement.

"The accidental dharma" isn't really an accident, it only appears like one. It's more like a surprise dharma.

Pros:

- The accidental dharma is your destiny—you were ushered into this situation because it was meant for you.
- There's a relative ease about your dharma because you never sought it, you just began embodying it.
- You don't have to figure it out and can just surrender to the natural process.

Cons:

- You can't set out to find an accidental dharma.
- It's often not what you *thought* you wanted to do— it's what you are *called* to do.
- May be a complete 180 from where you were before and you feel like you're starting from scratch again.

Regardless of your approach, you'll need to have some courage to take consistent action to fulfill your dharma. There will always be some kind of leap (which we will discuss later in the book), so there's no way to completely prevent any uncertainty. There are just ways to minimize it by planning ahead. However, not all of us are planners, and some of us learn in the free fall.

WHICH METHOD OF DISCOVERING YOUR DHARMA IS BEST FOR YOU?

I find you can instantly tell your approach to your dharma by the way you would write a book. There are multiple approaches to such an enormous topic, and your way of going about it will illustrate your relationship with your dharma.

If you were to write a book, would you:

A. Disconnect from everything for a period of time to focus only on your book?

B. Write a couple pages every morning or night?

C. Write whenever your creativity hits?

If you answered A, you're the kind of person who will fully commit to your dharma and cut off everything else. You are passionate, committed, and willing to do anything to get the job done, including cutting down on social media, Netflix, brunches, etc. Your dharma is an extension of who you are—there is no separation between you and your work. You can easily fall out of balance by throwing yourself into your work, and have to work on remembering other aspects of your life. (This is me! I'm so passionate about self-care because I often need to remind myself of its importance.)

This is the leap. You're an all-or-nothing person and thrive in that pressure to make things happen. You don't like to settle and always go all-in. You're willing to sacrifice the short-term for the benefit of the long-term and you know that distractions will always show up if you don't take active measures to create boundaries. If you haven't taken the leap yet, I highly advise that you do—with that fiery Pitta willpower, you'd rock it! Just be mindful not to overexert yourself, especially under an impending dead-line. It can be all too easy to put self-care, proper nutrition, exer-cise, and community on the shelf while focusing on your dharma. But the truth is, we need all of those things to truly embody our dharma. Continue to make time for yourself and prioritize the essentials that fuel you. Combine your needs, such as taking a walk with a friend to catch up so you're getting some movement in at the same time, or cooking a meal with your partner.

If you answered B, you are a balanced person who believes that slow and steady wins the race. You are committed to your daily obligations, whether it's your kids or your job, and often that comes before following your dharma. You're extremely realistic and only add changes into your life that are gradual and sustain-able. However, you can be slow to change, which is related to Kapha (earth) energy. The projects you've been working on can stagnate because you give only so much of yourself at a time. You find it tough to get your visions off the ground because you're lacking in momentum. It's also easy for daily obligations to get in the way of actually finding the time to commit to your dharma, forcing you to go around in circles.

This is the transition. You're someone who takes persistent action, which can make the transition possible for you. You don't feel like you're in the place to fully commit to working on your dharma and are living a double life—your "job" and your pas-sion. You are longing for the day that your weekend work can be your weeklong work. With your commitment to waking up early or trading couch time for dharma time, you'll be able to take your dharma off the ground running while still working full-time, so that you can transition into your dharma with ease. However, make sure you keep prioritizing that time. An hour in the mornings can easily slip on the weekends. Stick to your routine the way you would to brushing your teeth: It's just something you do.

If you answered C, you are a heart-centered person who likes to go where your intuition takes you. You don't like to set plans or make rules. When the creativity is there, you'll follow and if not, you won't chase it. You aren't desperate to make it happen, and rather let it come to you in due time. You follow the flow and see where life takes you.

That's accidental dharma. You're someone who likes to be guided and doesn't like to force things. You go with the flow until there's enough pain that it's no longer flowing. This is related to Vata (air) and Kapha (earth) energies. However, the shadow side of this is that "inspiration" may never come—you have to go find it. If you don't actively make time to dive into your gifts and clarify what it is you really want, you'll never be handed the opportunity on a silver plate. It's important for you to be proactive and initiate your dharma so the universe can support your efforts. Sometimes the only way to get a creative hit is to sit down and start writing.

As you can see, one approach isn't necessarily better than another—each has its own strengths and faults. Some people are naturally more all-in, while others are more gradual. The same book could be written at the end of the process, whether it's two months of going all-in, two years of writing early in the morning, or however long it takes. It's all up to you and your unique style. It's as if you choose to do a HIIT workout where you go all-in for thirty minutes, or a low-impact workout for sixty minutes, or just move whenever you feel inspired. You have to find what works for you.

Discovering Your Dharma Takes *Prioritizing* Your Dharma

If I were to look at your schedule and tell you how much you care about your dharma based only on that, how would I rank you? If you were in a relationship with dharma, would she be complaining about how you never spend time with her? Let's be real. Most of us don't spend nearly as much time with dharma as she needs to unfold and blossom. When we don't give our partners the attention they need and deserve, they become resentful. Ignoring your dharma for too long can feel like that, too. **Your dharma will only unfold when you make her a priority.**

The universe responds to wherever we put our energy. Look, I get it. It's not that you don't *want* to work on your dharma, it's that you have this thing that takes up your entire life called a job. And when you aren't working, you have a million errands to run, texts to respond to, emails to get back to, phone calls to delay (because we know we're not actually ever gonna do that). With all the things that come with life, dharma can get lost in the shuffle.

Even if you don't know what your dharma is, it's time you dedicate yourself to figuring it out. Sign up for an improv class or learn about online business or start vlogging weekly or read related books. We won't discover our dharmas when we are doing the same thing, day in and day out. Like dating, you gotta kiss a few frogs before you find your dharma. By making your discovery your priority, you expedite your path.

I know what you're thinking. "But I'm *so* busy." I hear you. I almost got too busy to write this book with my very full work life/getting married/moving/speaking/traveling/life things until I asked this very important question: "WTF *actually* matters?" If I were to die next year, what do I *actually* want to leave in the world? The proudest accomplishments in my life are my books. They're the thing I'm going to write home about when I'm a spirit guide, just to see how they're still landing on the human plane. So why wasn't I prioritizing my writing?

I took a piece of paper, drew a massive triangle, and wrote "Priority Triangle" on top. On the tip of the triangle, I wrote, "Write book." On the sides of the triangle, I wrote, "Plan Rose Gold Goddesses launch" and "Record podcasts." I continued as I went down the triangle, in order of priority, the top being my ride or die and the bottom being "It can wait another day/week." (Organizing my closet was somewhere down there.) I put this piece of paper next to my laptop and, every time I caught myself on Pinterest, I looked at it. Does this highly curated feed of boho chic apartments and messy braids help me write my book? No. There is a time and place for Pinterest vision-boarding, but when we prioritize that over making our lives our vision board, neither of them ever becomes our reality.

Prioritizing your dharma may look like an hour a day, a full day a week, early mornings, late nights, whatever floats your boat! But it means it is on and poppin', and you aren't going to ghost.

So I want to know:

WTF actually matters to you?

What do you love to do but don't have time for?

What does prioritizing your dharma look like for you?

What will happen if you don't prioritize your dharma?

What will happen if you do?

What will you need to cut back on to create space?

PS: I guarantee you there is more scrolling happening than you're admitting.

What are you going to tell yourself when excuses come up?

DISCOVER YOUR DHARMA MEDITATION/ JOURNAL EXERCISE

Discovering your dharma is not about going somewhere and finding something. It is not outside of you but rather it arises from going within. You already know your dharma. What we are going to do now is help you remember. This takes unraveling, unlearning, unconditioning—letting go of everything you are not so you can step into who you truly are.

In this meditation/journaling exercise, I'll be beginning a series of sentences that I'd like your intuition to complete. Don't use your rationality or write what you think should be the right answer. Allow your higher self to channel through. Without controlling, simply surrender and witness anything that comes to thought. Remember that your spirit talks to you through your own voice, so even if it seems like you're just thinking these things, you are in fact channeling. Just go with that first thing that comes along.

I recommend doing this meditation with me in my free guided meditation audio recording. You can download it at discoveryourdharmabook.com. You can also read this meditation here and write the answers in a journal.

I invite you to get a pen and paper, take a seat, close your eyes, and notice your breath. Observe its pace. Feel it expand and retract your chest. Feel it flow through your body. Connect with every inhale and exhale. Slowly lengthen the inhale, counting to seven, pause at the top and hold for four, and exhale out for seven counts. Repeat this for several minutes, until you can feel your body soften. Inhale seven, hold four, exhale seven.

Silently say in your mind, "I'd like to speak to the part of me that knows. Calling in the part of me that knows." Stay with the breath for several more minutes until you feel open to receive.

Once you feel ready, open your eyes and read these sentences out loud. Write the first thing that comes to mind.

> Right now I wish I was . . .
> The time I feel in my highest joy is . . .
> If I could make anything it would be . . .
> I find myself constantly telling people about . . .
> I love to help people with . . .
> I'd love to spend a month just . . .
> I fear . . .
> I want to leave this world more . . .
> I am ready to . . .

Did any answers surprise you? How did that make you feel? Did you draw a lot of blanks? Perhaps the message was loud and clear or perhaps you'll need to come back to this practice again to remember. Many are surprised by their answers and that is fantastic—you have just reached a new level of awareness because you have given yourself a moment to answer these questions. Others feel like they knew their answers all along, and that's awesome, too—you already know what's up! Some find it challenging to answer these questions and that's OK—your mind just may not be letting you hear them. Keep coming back to these questions as the answers continue to reveal. The more expansive questions you ask, the more expansive a person you become.

A QUICK RUNDOWN
FOR YOU SKIMMERS

It's not just one, two, three, dharma! There are many paths to get there. Some prefer that jump-off-a-cliff-into-a-waterfall rush; others prefer a transition where they slowly get their feet wet; others just somehow accidentally end up swimming without even knowing how they got there. All are valid. Trust what feels right for you.

You can't know your dharma without knowing yourself, so instead of stressing, put your energy toward asking yourself the real questions, like "WTF actually matters?" and "How do I want to spend my time?" Then your dharma will reveal itself. Your soul already knows what's up. It just takes your mind to allow you to hear the answers.

5

Doshas + Dharma

After spending years researching and writing about Ayurveda, the world's oldest health system and the sister science of yoga, I realized the Doshas and the Ayurvedic archetypes tell us about so much more than our health. They inform us of our dharmas.

I came to Ayurveda because of my massive Vata imbalance that caused my body to essentially shut down. But what I left with was a clear purpose to my life, healing my body on a deeper level than just food ever could.

Our minds and bodies are related and reflections of our spirit. Anything that is happening to us on a physical or emotional level is a reflection of what is happening inside. We experience certain imbalances, such as anxiety, irritation, depression, or even bloating and acidity, because of what is happening on a deeper soul level. Our bodies are constantly speaking to us, telling us what we need to focus on. When we look at our bodies as compasses for our truth, everything shifts. We realize that the answers we've been seeking weren't outside of us at all but rather are reflected in the vessels we reside in.

The word *Dosha* means "energy" in Sanskrit. Doshas are the three energy types based on the five elements. Vata = air + space, Pitta = fire + water, and Kapha = earth + water. To keep it simple, just think:

VATA = AIR

PITTA = FIRE

KAPHA = EARTH

since those are their most prominent elements.

We were each born with our own combination of all three Doshas for a reason—because it offers us the exact strengths, interests, and innate talents we need to fulfill our dharmas. Source made the painter more creative, the entrepreneur more ambitious, the life coach more compassionate. We need those Doshas because they cause us to naturally gravitate to the ways we were meant to serve. If you are looking for your Doshas, this chapter will help you understand that they are already inside of you.

I see the world through the lens of the Doshas, and in this book I will help you to put on your Dosha lens and see all the magnificent patterns in the world, too.

Vata is the energy of air—quick, fast-moving, unpredictable, cold. If I told you to think about an airy person, what would come to mind? Most likely you'll think about someone who wears eclectic clothes, has five careers going on at once, and flakes on your date. We even have related words in our English language—space cadet, airhead, airy fairy. This shows our understanding of qualities of air within the personality. But a Vata isn't just a hipster on Venice Beach. A Vata person is creative, artistic, visionary, ever-changing, connected to spirit, and often thinks outside the box. They are connected to the intangible, always coming up with new ideas. They're the ones who are always ahead of trends—they may seem crazy at first, but a couple years later, everyone wants to learn from them.

But the shadow side of this Dosha (and each has one) is that sometimes they may have so many ideas swirling through their head they don't know what to focus on. Their thoughts can circulate like a tornado, causing anxiety and insomnia. They're really good at starting projects, but not so good at finishing them. They live life with a million tabs open on their browser at once, causing their energy to be scattered. One day they're passionate about one thing, and the next they're totally over it. Every time you meet them, it's like meeting a new person. They may struggle with commitment and actually putting in the work to getting their dharma done. My highest advice for them is to ground and anchor (trust me, I used to be super Vata).

Think about someone who is inspiring to you. Maybe they're a spiritual teacher, writer, artist, astrologer, designer, or musician. They have a way of channeling their ideas with ease and fluidity. They're always crafting up new visions and using imagery and words to bring them to life. This is an example of a Vata—inspirational, creative, artistic, open, channeling Source.

Pitta is fire energy—sharp, transformational, direct, hot. If I told you to think of a fiery person, what comes to mind? Most likely you'd think about a feisty person with a bit of a temper who you wouldn't want to cross. We have a word for it in English—a hothead—and can imagine the fire coming out of their ears. Well, that fiery person isn't always angry. Pittas are ambitious, determined, entrepreneurial, and organized. They know what they want and they're going to go get it. They have a lot of energy that they choose to direct toward their goals. They're natural leaders and adept at taking ideas off the ground and into the world. They're the type of person who will send you a Google Cal to confirm your walk together from 2:12–4:43 and request a twenty-four-hour confirmation.

The shadow side of this Dosha is that sometimes with all that fire energy, they can snap. There are times when life doesn't go your way (anyone else?) and a person flakes on you without hitting No on Google Cal, completely ruining your schedule, and this is when the fire can erupt into a volcano. Pittas can be impatient, judgmental, or bossy and must work with going with the flow. My mantra for them is "Trust and surrender."

Think about someone who is really motivational for you. Maybe they're an entrepreneur, an author, a professional, or an athlete. Hearing them speak lights a fire under your ass and makes you want to go out and chase your dreams. Their drive motivates you to up yours and commit to living your dharma. This is an example of a Pitta—fierce, fiery, and ferocious.

Kapha is earth energy—grounded, anchored, slow, cool. If I told you to think of an earthy person, what comes to mind? Maybe you imagine someone with their shoes off, in a flowing dress and long hair, walking in nature, playing the ukulele while breastfeeding their kid? We even say "earth mama" to describe this person. Well, Kaphas aren't just tree huggers. Kaphas are empathic, loving, giving, humorous, and good-natured. If you think about the Earth, she always provides, no matter how much we take, and that is the energy Kaphas have. They are natural nurturers and love to make people around them feel comfortable and special. They're the type of people who will remember someone's birthday and send them a sweet note, or listen to a complete stranger vent about their problems for an hour while empathically nodding along, truly listening. Their grounded nature makes them excellent coaches, therapists, customer service specialists, HR directors, teachers, nurses, and caregivers. They are very in touch with other people's needs and can remain centered even when people around them are frazzled.

The shadow side of this Dosha is sometimes they give so much that they end up trying to pour from an empty cup. Boundaries are difficult for them, and they can often say yes when they mean no. They want to be there for everyone else but feel like they may not have anyone to talk to about what is going on within themselves. Because they are taking on so many other people's energies, they need to get energy in from somewhere, which often leads to emotional/binge eating. This causes them to feel heavy and lethargic, keeping them from exercising and trying new things, perpetuating the Kapha cycle. My mantra for them is "Release the expectation of others and love yourself first."

Think about someone who immediately makes you calm. Maybe it's a friend, a relative, a coach/therapist, or a content creator. Somehow they always know just what to say. Hearing their voice immediately makes you exhale a little deeper. They have a way of pouring honey into your heart and sweetening up your soul. This is an example of a Kapha—kind, loving, and joyous.

You are a combination of all three Doshas, but in varying amounts. This is called your Doshic constitution. You may be primarily a Vata, secondarily a Kapha, lastly a Pitta, or any other combination. One of your Doshas may be prevalent, or all three may be fairly close to equal. You were born with this array of the three Doshas, which is called your *prakriti*, your natural-born constitution. This constitution is never-changing and is related to your dharma.

However, your Doshas can shift and fall out of balance throughout your life, depending on your lifestyle, diet, stress levels, etc. For example, you may have been born a creative Vata who loved to draw as a kid, but because of pressure from your parents, you focused on achieving grades and career success, which caused you to become more Pitta. You may have ridden the Pitta waves for a while until you found yourself completely fried. You look back and remember the times you were happiest, and they're when you were just creating—something you never give yourself a chance to do. Your Pitta is in excess for your unique physiology, causing your burnout. It's time for you to come back to your creative Vata nature.

Or perhaps you were born more Pitta and were always playing sports as a kid, but after having kids of your own you stopped exercising, put on a lot of weight, and became sluggish and depressed. You may think you are a Kapha, but you just have a Kapha imbalance—you must go back to your fiery Pitta nature to shake off the extra energy you're holding onto.

Or perhaps you were born more Kapha and were always playing house and taking care of animals as a child. However, you moved to a big city and ended up not having time to go slow and do the things you love. You find yourself scattered, forgetting things. You may think you are a Vata, but you just have a Vata imbalance—you must go back to your grounded Kapha nature to regain the sweetness of who you are.

The key to fulfilling our dharma is to reclaim the Doshic constitution we were born with. Essentially, your only job is to be you, exactly as you are. Source created you this way so you could fulfill your sacred mission here. We don't want fiery therapists or spacey managers or slow-moving trainers. We want people to truly embody who they are—and can feel when they are not. The Doshas help you put language to the observations and patterns you've been noticing about people your entire life but just didn't have the vocabulary for. Now that you know the Doshas, you're going to be seeing the world through this new lens (don't say I didn't warn ya!).

In this book, we'll be focusing on how the Doshas are related to your dharma, but they go so much deeper than that—I've written two books on Ayurveda (*Eat Feel Fresh* and *Idiot's Guide to Ayurveda*) that tell you everything you need to know about Ayurvedic science, nutrition, self-care, and spiritual and lifestyle practices (don't say I didn't warn ya!).

I invite you to take my ninety-second quiz to assess your unique Doshic constitution. This quiz will give you the exact percentages of each Dosha you have in both your mind and your body, as well as customized videos and a minicourse with suggestions on how to bring your Doshas back into balance. You can take the quiz at iamsahararose.com.

I've created the quiz below to assess what your Dosha is in relation to your dharma, which is a unique finding I discovered that hasn't been taught before. I believe these Doshas can inform us in every aspect of our lives, from our dharma to our relationships to our businesses, and it's part of my dharma to deliver this work to the world. I'm honored to be sharing with you.

What's Your Dosha + Dharma?

Choose the answer that best describes you.

1. What are your strengths?

A. My creativity and ability to think outside the box. I'm constantly coming up with new ideas!

B. My dedication and ability to make things happen. I can take my vision off the ground and into the world.

C. My sensitivity and compassion. I can sense exactly how someone is feeling and hold space for people's emotions.

2. I'm that person you call when . . .

A. You want to talk about the meaning of life, art, aliens, or the new moon.

B. You have a business question and want no-BS advice.

C. You need someone to vent to who can just hear you out without judging.

3. What's your work life like?

A. I do best when I have lots of different projects going on to keep me entertained and on my toes!

B. I do best when I'm focused on a goal and have a team around to support me.

C. I do best working one-on-one, getting really deep with someone, or using my hands by cooking or making crafts.

4. In times of stress I . . .

A. Get anxious, overwhelmed, and try to run away! Escapism is my go-to.

B. Get impatient, irritated, and sometimes snap. The frustration really gets to me!

C. Get sad and suppress my emotions, causing me to emotionally eat and withdraw.

5. I'm great at . . .

A. Beginning projects, creating visions, crafting words, inventing ideas.

B. Taking an idea to action, creating solutions, making it profitable, and having an impact.

C. Inviting people to open up to me, being sensitive to people's triggers, making a beautiful home.

6. I feel happiest when I'm . . .

A. Creating, visualizing, free-flowing, traveling, daydreaming, making art.

B. Leading, making money, building my business, sharing my mission, and making an impact.

C. Connecting deeply, relaxing, spending time with people I love, making meals.

7. As a child I could be found . . .

A. Drawing, playing with my imaginary friends, making up skits, dressing up.

B. Running around outside, playing sports, winning in board games, climbing trees.

C. Playing house, taking care of animals/dolls, talking to friends for hours, reading books.

8. Which chakra is your most powerful?

    A. Third eye and throat—I have a unique ability to see visions and express them.

    B. Solar plexus—I am confident, empowered, and quick to take action.

    C. Heart—I feel deeply, and this is my superpower.

9. People come to me ...

    A. When they need help coming up with creative ideas.

    B. When they need help with specific solutions.

    C. When they need help with personal issues.

10. I prefer to work ...

    A. By myself, freely, at random times without a schedule.

    B. With a dynamic team who supports and understands the mission.

    C. One-on-one, in a peaceful office or alone, calmly.

11. Which animal do you relate to most?

    A. A butterfly—always in metamorphosis, unique, beautiful.

    B. A lion—fierce, courageous, strong.

    C. An elephant—compassionate, loving, gentle.

12. My dharma definitely ...

    A. Uses my unique visions to create something the world has never seen before.

    B. Is a mission far greater than me where we make lots of money and give lots away.

    C. Allows me to be of service to others and gives me space for self-care.

13. I'm willing to forgo . . .

    A. Profits or comfort to honor my creativity.

    B. Freedom or comfort to honor my determination.

    C. Profit or freedom to honor my comfort.

14. Which careers sound most appealing to you?

    A. Author, artist, spiritual teacher, mystic, inventor, fashion/graphic designer, astrologer

    B. Entrepreneur, CEO, motivational speaker, fitness professional, lawyer, doctor

    C. Life coach, therapist, healer, novelist, chef, interior designer, teacher, energy worker

Count up your answers.

A = VATA

B = PITTA

C = KAPHA

About Each Dosha

VATA, THE AIR DOSHA

You are an idealistic visionary who thinks outside the box and inspires others to do the same. Creativity is your superpower. You love getting lost in conversation and going down rabbit holes on the secrets of the universe. You are someone who requires a lot of freedom because you are constantly changing—every time people see you, it's as if they are meeting a new iteration of who you are. You are constantly reinventing yourself and go through many phases as you uncover what you truly want. You get extremely excited about starting new projects—but aren't as good at finishing them because another feels more exciting.

With all this air flowing through your mind, your thoughts can sometimes spiral into a tornado, leaving you feeling anxious, overwhelmed, and scattered. You bounce around different tabs on your browser (literally and figuratively) and have a hard time seeing things to completion. It's important for you to harness your Pitta (fire) energy so the world can experience your wisdom.

YOUR DHARMA

To bring inspiration, creativity, art, and/or beauty into this world

PITTA, THE FIERY DOSHA

You are an ambitious, driven individual who is dedicated to making positive change in this world. You put your money where your mouth is, and the money keeps growing because of it! You keep slaying your goals, then setting even bigger ones, because that's the boss you are. You are someone who needs to know where they are going. You live for your quarterly goals, a color-coordinated Google Cal, a clean inbox, and surpassing your projected income. Productivity is your meditation. You feel best when you're getting shit done and getting paid for your hard work because you know that helps you make the biggest impact, which is why you're here.

With all this fire in your mind, it can be hard for you to turn off the Pitta and take a rest. Your quest for perfectionism can lead you to taking on too much. You can forget to be human for too long, leading to burnout, adrenal fatigue, irritability, and agitation. It's important for you to take action, then take a break so you can allow the next idea to come through without pushing it.

YOUR
DHARMA

To bring great ideas and innovations to life so they can create impact while being profitable

KAPHA, THE EARTH DOSHA

You are an empathic, generous soul who lives for deep, meaningful connections. It's normal for someone to share with you secrets they haven't told anyone before because they pick up on your anchored energy. You have a soothing, nurturing presence and are the person your friends come to whenever they need a shoulder to lean on. You love working with your hands and enjoy cooking, crafting, or designing, and you make personal details that touch people's hearts. You know you aren't meant to sacrifice your inner peace for the sake of your dharma—your dharma comes through when you feel at peace. You don't feel the need to hustle like other people and prefer to live a comfortable life with healthy relationships.

With all this earth in your mind, you can get too stuck in your comfort zone. You may avoid taking the action you know you need to because it can feel exhausting and overwhelming. You focus completely on your daily responsibilities and not on taking the initiative to sign up for a new program, quit that job, exercise, or launch that business. It's important for you to set boundaries, try something new, take a risk, and shake things up a bit so your dharma can come through.

YOUR DHARMA

To connect with people and show them the love that is inside of them

Remember, you aren't just one but a combination of all three, which may show up in different areas of your life. We classify ourselves by our primary and secondary Doshas. You may be a Vata-Kapha, Pitta-Kapha, or Vata-Pitta. A Vata-Pitta can come up with ideas (Vata), as well as the strategy to execute them (Pitta). However, they probably aren't the best at customer service, because their energy is quick-moving and can come across as harsh. A Vata-Kapha has the imagination of a Vata and the groundedness of a Kapha but may have a difficult time taking action on their visions (Pitta). A Pitta-Kapha may have a lot of energy (Pitta) and the endurance to stick with their goals (Kapha), but may lack the creativity to know what it is they need to focus on (Vata).

VATA-PITTA/PITTA-VATA DHARMA:
To channel ideas and bring them to life

They love the freedom of working alone while also thriving on the energy of others in a collaborative environment with a shared goal.

Careers that can manifest as:
Coach that inspires (Vata) and motivates (Pitta) people
Entrepreneur, business professional
Marketing/social media/branding professional

Fitness/yoga professional
Motivational/inspirational content creator, speaker, author
Teacher, expert
Example: Myself, Gabby Bernstein

VATA-KAPHA/KAPHA-VATA DHARMA:
To channel ideas that help people

They crave alone time, as well as working directly with people; they must have a good balance of connecting with others while taking time to recharge.

Careers that can manifest as:

Coach that inspires (Vata) and connects (Kapha) with people
Small business owner of self-made product
Self-love/authenticity content creator, speaker, author, editor
Meditation/yoga teacher
Wedding/event coordinator
Example: Brené Brown

PITTA-KAPHA/KAPHA-PITTA DHARMA:
To bring projects that help people to life

They love to execute projects where they are helping others and like a good mix of systems and heartfelt connection.

Careers that can manifest as:

Coach that motivates (Pitta) and connects (Kapha) with people
Body-worker, energy healer, acupuncturist, herbalist
Mind-body/meditation content creator, speaker, author
Chef, artisan, small business owner
Project manager, human resources manager, community manager
Example: Deepak Chopra

You can build your dharma around your Dosha—in fact, that's the only way to make it sustainable!

The Dosha Cycle to Discovering Your Dharma

Now that we know the Doshas, I'd like to share with you how they work as a compass to navigating our dharma. Once I was on a panel and was asked how someone can create a business doing what they love, and suddenly the answer arose. Through the Doshas. Not only do we have the Doshas inside us, but what I've realized is even our dharmas go through the three phases of the Doshas. Each phase has its own characteristics and is essential for your dharma to come through. You can think of it like cycles of the moon, each of which needs to happen for the next one to appear. These Doshic cycles repeat as we fine-tune and expand our dharmas.

THEY ARE CATEGORIZED IN THREE STAGES
Vata = The Idea Phase
Pitta = The Execution Phase
Kapha = The Reevaluation Phase

Many people remain in the Vata phase of their dharma for this entire lifetime. They keep thinking of ideas but never take action on them. And then they wonder why their dreams never came true! If you remain in the Vata phase for too long, you'll inevitably talk yourself out of your dharma. However, when you commit to something, your mental energy shifts into Pitta and becomes more focused on how you can improve what you're doing, instead of finding something else. It's taking that business idea you always talk about and actually writing a plan for how you're going to make it happen.

Often, we don't take this pause in the Pitta phase because there's so much going on and things are expanding so quickly, but if we don't choose our breaks, our breaks will choose us. You may get a fever or burn out, both related to excess fire. Your best ideas never happen when you're on your laptop, frustrated and exhausted, trying to figure out how to solve an issue. It's when you take a step back and don't think about it for a hot second that the answers come through.

In this phase, you've changed significantly from when you first began the Vata phase, and now your life needs another evaluation. Perhaps what you're doing is no longer in alignment with the next evolution of your dharma. Perhaps you're feeling depleted because you put all of your Pitta energy into your dharma. Restoration can only come through Kapha, when we trade progress for slowness and remember what it means to be human. Kapha allows us to check back in with our internal compass and see where we want to set our sails.

Some people stay in this phase forever because it feels so comfortable. It removes the pressure of having to *do* anything and allows for a lot of self-compassion. While this is a beautiful phase to be in, it's still just a phase. Its purpose is to act as the springboard to bring you back to your next idea, the Vata stage, as we begin the cycle again. We don't buy a comfortable mattress to stay in bed forever, right? We rest so we can rise. The Kapha phase is there to nourish your body and soul so that you can get back there with an even higher perspective. From this deep space of recharging, you'll naturally spring forth with new ideas, beginning the Vata stage again with a more refined vision on how you'll serve.

Vata = The Idea Phase
Brainstorming
Visualizing
Big-picture thinking

Questions during this phase:
What do I want?
What do I enjoy?
What could doing that every day look like?
What are some ways to get there?

Pitta = The Execution Phase
Strategizing
Action steps
Delivering

Questions during this phase:
How can I grow?
How can I automate and streamline aspects of my business?
How can I set up support structures?
How can I expand this vision?

Kapha = The Reevaluation Phase
Resting
Reevaluating
Making shifts

Questions during this phase:
How can I use what I've learned to improve in the future?
How can I tap back into my passion?
How can I make this more aligned with my current desires?
How can I let this have its own legs, to live on without me?

It's important to remember that all stages are essential for any dharma. Without the Vata stage, you won't have a strong vision of what your dharma is. Without the Pitta stage, you won't execute anything, and it will remain just an idea. Without the Kapha stage, you'll burn out and end up achieving a goal that is meaningless to you. Some of us naturally remain in the Vata stage, others in the Pitta, and others in the Kapha, depending on our Dosha. However, tapping into all three is essential for fulfilling our ultimate dharma.

We're All Different

We are all in the constant process of moving our dharma through the Doshas, each of which represents a unique and significant stage in our creation process. We all have to come up with the idea, act upon it, and reevaluate it. In this way, the Doshas are universal.

However, our personal combination of the Doshas reveals itself by lingering in a specific phase. Someone who is naturally more Vata-centric will love the idea phase. They can come up with a brand name faster than you can sneeze, and they get excited at the prospect of beginnings. However, the implementation phase is more challenging for them—how to actually get those ideas off the ground and into real life, dealing with the day in, day out repetition when things don't feel as exciting or novel anymore. It's important to break things down step by step: What is the first step toward making this idea a reality, and what can be done next? Anyone in the Vata phase will become overwhelmed by the enormity of their dharma if they don't break it down into bite-size pieces. For someone who is more Vata-minded, this might be a challenge, and they may need to seek help from someone who's more Pitta-minded to help them organize and execute their visions.

Someone who is naturally more Pitta-centric will love the "get shit done" phase. Before they've even properly formulated the idea, they're already itching to do it. They get excited about the prospect of creating and are quick to take the first leap. While often beneficial, it can also hurt them, because their action may be hasty and not thought out. Instead of moving them forward, it can sometimes take them a few steps back. Pittas can also get so deep in the doing that they forget about their why. They don't always step back and ask themselves, "Is this still aligned with who I am today?" It can be the greatest challenge to step away from a fully fledged business that needs your constant care and attention. But if you don't periodically do it, you'll continue regurgitating a former version of yourself. Pittas need to step into the Kapha mindset to ask themselves how they can share their gifts in an even grander way. Sometimes that takes support from a Kapha friend or colleague to remind them to chill, take it easy, and look at the big picture. Pittas always want to execute the best ideas, but those ideas only come when you create space in Kapha mode.

Someone who's naturally more Kapha-centric will love the restorative part of the dharma. They want to connect with the people whose lives they've touched, which can benefit them because they're extremely aware of client needs, customer service, and personal connections. It can also hurt them because they're so caught up in how other people feel that they don't pursue what *they* truly want. For example, the Kapha may be concerned about how their family will feel if they pursue their dharma and feel too bad about putting themselves first. As caring and compassionate as they are, they need to show that same love to themselves. Kaphas must understand that it's not selfish to follow your dharma. In fact, it's the *only* responsibility you have on this planet. You can only be the parent/child/spouse/ friend you want to be when you're truly fulfilled on a soul level. Kaphas can feel overwhelmed by all the steps it takes to fulfill one's dharma and instead choose to stay exactly where they are. What isn't going to help is someone yelling at them to go do it—that can feel harsh and make them suppress even more. What Kaphas need is to dream: visualize what they want, what their dharma may be, and how their life will feel when they get there. They need to move into the Vata and surround themselves with Vata visionaries. From this place of inspiration, they will naturally want to take action.

As you can see, the Doshas are a beautiful cycle we all go through repeatedly as our dharma unfolds and unravels. Our natural-born Dosha just informs us of what stage we may be more drawn to and more prone to settle in—and it reminds us of where we need to go next.

If you're in the Vata idea phase—take action. Send an email. Write a plan. Just start doing it.

If you're in the Pitta execution phase—pull back. Take a walk. Take a breath. Take some time to calibrate and then come back from that point of higher alignment.

If you're in the Kapha reevaluation phase—dream. What do you want? How will it make you feel? You get to call the shots, so it's time for you to start visualizing the life that you're worthy of.

How to Deal with
Dharma Overwhelm

We've all been there—wanting our dharma so badly but also being overwhelmed by the process. Believe me, I feel you. But what I've observed is that there are three types of overwhelm, each related to a Dosha (I told you I see the world through this lens!).

VATA OVERWHELM

Do you ever have so many ideas that you have no idea where to start, and then end up feeling so overwhelmed that you end up doing nothing at all? That's Vata overwhelm. This is the most freeing and overwhelming stage, because anything is possible. You can run wild with ideas or let the ideas run you wild. This is the phase before you've actually taken action, so it's much easier to walk away.

Vata overwhelm is airy in quality. It makes you feel spacey, heady, cloudy, and confused. All the energy is in your mind, which can leave you feeling ungrounded. The air is always moving and so are your ideas, causing you to feel scattered and unsettled. Because Vata is air energy, it needs to transform through the fire—Pitta. That overwhelmed feeling won't just go away by ignoring it; you have to act upon it and bring it to clarity.

The only way to overcome the turbulence of your thoughts and contradictory ideas is to just start *doing* something, even if you aren't 100 percent sure about it. You'll know what's right for you only when you begin taking action. You can spend a lifetime debating whether or not you want to be a photographer, but it's only when you get your hands on a camera that you realize whether you actually enjoy it. A low-risk way to try a dharma on for size is to begin working/interning for someone who is vision-board material for you. This could be someone who is living a life similar to one you'd like to have or is showing up in the world in a way that inspires you. Working for this person will help you see the ins and outs of their career. You may be surprised by the different responsibilities, work hours, and ways they actually spend their time. Only through the experience can you decide whether it's something you do or do not aspire to have.

If it isn't the type of thing you could work on for someone else, then just start doing it yourself! This may mean putting your homemade candles on Etsy, selling your skin-care products at a local farmers market, publishing your website, or taking on some free clients to build your practice and get good reviews. We often wait for permission from someone else to tell us that we can begin following our dharma, but it really begins when we give *ourselves* permission. If you've been waiting for a permission slip, here it is.

You don't lose anything from taking action—you only gain experience. After all, is it better to live in the fantasy of a potential dharma or to give it a try and find yourself redirected to your true one? The only failure is stagnancy. When you put one foot in front of another, you're showing the universe that you care and are creating kriya in the direction of your dharma.

PITTA OVERWHELM

Have you ever had so much on your plate that you had no idea how you were going to get through the day? That's Pitta overwhelm. It doesn't come from not knowing what to do, like Vata overwhelm. It comes from having so much to do that you don't know how you can do it all. Part of you wants to jump right into it, and the other part wants to run away to Bali. This is *classic* Pitta overwhelm.

And, because its nature is so different from Vata, it needs to be handled differently. Pitta overwhelm is fiery. It makes you feel hot, sweaty, and uncomfortable, whereas Vata overwhelm makes you feel spacey and cloudy. When Pitta overwhelm hits, you feel the energy moving through your body and want to take action, even blindly. This can lead to mistakes and eventual burnout.

We often try to rationalize our Pitta overwhelm by saying that we need to work this hard or we won't get everything done, but it's just an illusion. Your career will not collapse without your relentless presence—it will expand. It's important to build a team with trustworthy people around you to take some of that stress away so you can focus on making the big decisions.

When you experience that Pitta overwhelm, the first thing you must do is create space by taking a Kapha pause. Observe the sensations in your body. How are you breathing? Where is your tension being held? Simply by observing, you begin removing yourself from the experience and become its witness. "I feel tension in my head, my body feels hot, my shoulders feel tight, my breath is shallow." Simply by analyzing how you feel, you begin calming down because you've created the separation between yourself and your current state. When we witness our sensations, we no longer identify with them as strongly. We move from the victim to the observer. This is exactly what we need to do when the Pitta overwhelm kicks in.

Something to remember in Pitta overwhelm is that scientists have found that taking six deep breaths is the exact number we need to calm the nervous system. Allow your shoulders to drop and roll backward. We somatically carry the weight of the world on our shoulders, so simply by releasing tension in our shoulders we can drop some of that accumulated stress. Now reach your arms up and stretch. Creating space in your physical body creates space in your mind. When we clear stagnant energy physically, we clear it mentally. I also recommend circling your hips, connecting you to your sacral and root chakras, grounding your energy and reconnecting you to the divine feminine, which is a softer, more yin energy. Take a stroll outside and connect to nature, as looking at the color green helps calm the nervous system. Though walking away from your to-do list may sound counterintuitive, your best work isn't going to come through when you're overwhelmed. Practicing embodiment (breath and movement) will take you out of your head and bring you back home into your body, where you feel rooted, grounded, and in control. Stress doesn't exist outside of you—it's a state within. The world cannot stress you out if you are not stressed out. As you detach yourself from stress, you'll start to observe yourself not reacting to situations that would've triggered you before.

Avoid intellectualizing your overwhelm. Being in the mind will not combat being in the mind. You have to get back into the body. When you catch yourself in the Pitta overwhelm, make it your practice to move into the Kapha, even when it feels like the last thing you should be doing. It will always make you vibrate from an even higher frequency.

KAPHA OVERWHELM

Have you ever felt like you just don't have the energy it takes to fulfill your dharma? You see what needs to be done, but your body just can't get itself to physically do it. You look at other people buzzing around like bees and you feel more like a sloth. That's the Kapha overwhelm. But, to move past this inertia, remember this: Energy creates energy. A dharma in motion stays in motion.

We don't get energy by lying on the couch—it just makes us drowsier. It's like exercise: People often make the excuse that they can't work out because they don't have the energy, but working out is what *gives* you the energy, as counterintuitive as it sounds. It's the same principle here. You don't need endless energy to do your dharma; doing your dharma gives you endless energy.

So how do you get energy when you don't have any? Remind yourself of how you'll feel afterward, when you've finally gotten your website up or are working with your first client or whatever will mean you're living a life with purpose. Remind yourself of those feelings—empowered, grateful, proud, accomplished, peaceful, inspired—and they will help you take action. Compare those feelings with how you feel now: overwhelmed, exhausted, scared, intimidated. How would you prefer to feel?

Another form of Kapha overwhelm is the feeling of obligation and resentment that comes from the expectations of others. Have you ever been offended by something that someone has asked you to do but not expressed it to them? That's Kapha overwhelm in the form of not having clear boundaries. In life, people ask for things. They're not wrong for asking; we're wrong for giving when it's not authentic for us. We can't get mad that someone crossed a boundary we didn't set—especially if we've continually said yes in the past.

For example, you may have a habit of making yourself available for phone calls with a friend so that she can vent about her personal life for hours. The first couple of times you did it just to be a good friend, but now it's becoming a habit—every time she calls you, your body gets tense and your mind begins racing because you know she's about to offload on you. But you still pick up. Maybe you're trying to not pick up as often or be shorter on the phone, but you haven't clearly drawn that boundary. If you're not sure about it, how can she be? We get overwhelmed by the expectations of others when we allow ourselves to put their needs above our own. When we're clear about what we can and cannot give, we don't let others' expectations overwhelm us. And it feels empowering.

A QUICK RUNDOWN
FOR YOU SKIMMERS

Looking for your dharma? Look no further than your Dosha! Vatas are the creative types; Pittas like to get shit done; Kaphas like to connect deeply. You are a combination of all three but in varying amounts. Your dharma goes through all three phases: Vata is the idea phase, Pitta is the execution, Kapha is the reevaluation. Whenever you're stuck, look at which Dosha is most prominent and that will inform you where to go next.

If you're Vata overwhelmed (too many ideas), take action. If you're Pitta overwhelmed (overworked), take a break. If you're Kapha overwhelmed (feeling stuck), dream big. The Doshas are your compass, always guiding you toward dharma.

6

Dharma Archetypes

Archetypal work has been instrumental in my life because it's allowed me to see the patterns in myself and others. Archetypes are as ancient as the Vedas and as universal as consciousness. They are personality types that have existed since the beginning of time, such as the mother or the wild woman. The Doshas, Goddesses, Jungian archetypes, Myers-Briggs, Enneagram, and Michael Teachings are archetypical systems, all of which reveal a new side of ourselves. Essentially they allow us to connect the dots and understand ourselves on a deeper level.

Through downloads from the universe, I received nine archetypes that are related to our dharma, which I call the Dharma Archetypes. We each have chosen these archetypes as souls to fulfill our life's work before incarnation. They allow us to excel at exactly what it is our dharma involves. They support our dharma by making it feel natural to us.

The Dharma Archetypes are the universal expressions of the soul types that exist within all of us, and have proven to be a crucial tool that's helped me to work through my own dharmic journey and guide others through theirs. Knowing your Dharma Archetype will help you understand why you are drawn to certain things and give you permission to fully step into the embodiment of who you are.

The Dharma Archetypes build off the Doshas but further categorize them into actual roles in our society. When you begin reading about the Dharma Archetypes, you'll likely recognize your friends, your family, and yourself instantly. These archetypes are all universal—you'll find them in Kenya, China, Peru, England, and any other part of the world, as our souls know no borders.

I believe that the universe encoded us with these unique Dharma Archetypes so that we can naturally come into balance as a whole society. If we all had the same personalities, gifts, and traits, there'd be no such thing as talent. If we all had the exact same capabilities, there'd be no such thing as an incredible singer or artist or healer or inventor. Everything would be the same, and therefore boring. The universe did not design you to be well-rounded like your school's college counselor may have told you; it designed you to be you.

I like to think of the universe playing *The Sims* when I think about the Dharma Archetypes. If you weren't a Sims nerd like I was, let me fill you in: In this epic computer game, you create your own humans and design their personalities before sticking them in a house together. You're able to decide how outgoing, organized, patient, active, or even flirtatious each person is going to be. (I always made one super-introverted with a love of organization so that he would keep the house clean. Code rosebud for tons of Sims money. You're welcome.) Just like The Sims, the universe designed us to have a variety of skills, interests, and talents so that together we can make the world whole. There is always someone who loves to do the things you despise. So why force yourself to fit into another person's shoes when you were meant to be the Sim that the universe created?

Now, let's get into the Dharma Archetypes specifically. Though you alone embody your unique expression, you share a similar archetype with others who were meant to do similar work, though in their own unique way. There are nine archetypes, and like the Doshas, we're generally a combination of all nine, in varying amounts. (This is *not* like one of those personality quizzes where only one result applies to you so you skip over the rest.) You can rank high in multiple archetypes, as well as low in more than one. One archetype may shine through, or two may be close to equal. Some of your archetypes may not have awakened and some may have already completed their role.

The more self-aware you become, the more your archetype will reveal. This is why meditative practices such as dance therapy, meditation, introspection, journaling, breathwork, sound baths, and plant medicine are so important—they open up aspects of our souls that we were not aware of yet. As you continue to read this book, your consciousness will expand, and your archetypes will become more and more clear to you.

Feel into each of the archetypes as you read the descriptions. Who comes to mind when you think about this archetype and how do you feel about them? Are there certain archetypes you know you were meant to embody but haven't yet? Do some feel totally foreign to you? This is feedback from your soul. It's normal to feel some tingling, shortness of breath, tears, excitement, or even fear as you read them. This comes from the reunion between you and your soul. Discovering your archetype is like coming back home.

For each archetype, I will explain the associated chakra balance. Chakras are energy centers up the base of the spine that represent various psychosomatic characteristics. I discuss chakras more deeply in Chapter 7.

If you have an "aha" moment, I suggest putting the book down and journaling what's coming up for you. We all fit under several of these archetypes, so don't worry about not finding "the one"—yours are in there, waiting for you to recognize them.

What's Your Dharma Archetype?

There are two ways to do this assessment: the detailed, nerdy way and the quick way. For the detailed way, rate your answer for each question nine to one, from which resonates with you most to least, nine being "That's so me!" and one being "That's not me." For the quick version, just choose the answer that resonates most from each category. Also, try not to overthink it; just go with whatever first comes to mind. And remember, this is in relation to your dharma. Your kids won't read your results.

1. What matters to you most?

A. ___ Improving the lives of others through valuable education

B. ___ My partner, family, and friends

C. ___ Raising the vibration of the planet

D. ___ Developing creative solutions to people's problems

E. ___ Making the world a more beautiful place

F. ___ Understanding why the world is the way it is

G. ___ Making people laugh, cry, and think

H. ___ Standing up for a just cause

I. ___ Protecting my friends, family, and the vulnerable

2. I am happiest:

A. ___ Teaching what I love

B. ___ Connecting deeply with someone

C. ___ Inspiring people to see a higher perspective

D. ___ Coming up with business ideas

E. ___ Creating art

F. ___ Deep in research

G. ___ On stage, on set, or at rehearsal

H. ___ Raising awareness on important causes

I. ___ Using my physical body

3. I like to spend my time

A. ___ Learning new things and then teaching them to others

B. ___ With my loved ones

C. ___ Channeling my realizations to others

D. ___ Masterminding business ideas

E. ___ Alone, surrounded by my art

F. ___ Going down rabbit holes and finding new conclusions

G. ___ Cracking jokes, writing skits, practicing lines

H. ___ Volunteering

I. ___ With my team, supporting each other toward our goals

4. At my best, I'm:

A. ____ Giving people "aha" moments

B. ____ Deeply connected to others

C. ____ Channeling higher visions to uplift humanity

D. ____ Creating solutions for people's problems

E. ____ A creative genius

F. ____ Understanding things people never even think about

G. ____ Uplifting everyone around me

H. ____ Making a massive difference on the planet

I. ____ Empowered, ignited, and ready to charge

5. At my worst I'm:

A. ____ Frustrated, trying to get people to understand something they cannot

B. ____ Resentful of people taking advantage of my kindness

C. ____ Anxious about the way the world is going

D. ____ Overworked and burned-out from my work

E. ____ Mad at myself for not doing better

F. ____ Upset with how uneducated people are and how little regard they have

G. ____ Depressed, falling into addictive behaviors

H. ____ Pissed that no one cares about the world like I do

I. ____ Angry, feeling like I've been fighting my entire life

6. People compliment me most on:

A. ____ My ability to make complicated topics easy to understand

B. ___ My compassion, patience, and kindness

C. ___ My intuition and ability to channel wisdom from Source

D. ___ My ability to create a business around anything, my resourcefulness

E. ___ My creativity and ability to think outside the box

F. ___ My deep knowledge and curiosity about the world

G. ___ My theatrical nature and ability to read a crowd

H. ___ My passion to help the world

I. ___ My strength and loyalty

A = TEACHER

B = NURTURER

C = VISIONARY

D = ENTREPRENEUR

E = ARTIST

F = RESEARCHER

G = ENTERTAINER

H = ACTIVIST

I = WARRIOR

Tally your answers here.

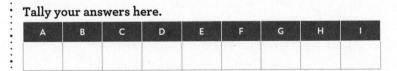

A	B	C	D	E	F	G	H	I

Teacher

PREDOMINANT DOSHAS: VATA + KAPHA

The Teacher is here to teach the experiences they undergo. They find the lesson in their human experience and share it with others. They'll write a social media post revealing their key takeaways and action steps for you to learn, too. They're the type of people who taught themselves how to make vegan desserts or launch successful online businesses, and are now teaching others to do the same. They learn through teaching, and everything they experience is understood through sharing it with others.

The Teacher's mission is to serve through knowledge. The obstacles they go through are exactly what they're meant to share with others, which is why most coaches are Teachers. The personal experience fills them with a genuine desire to teach what they've overcome. They are the type to see the lesson in an obstacle even as they are dealing with it, and use it as an example as they guide others through it. They have natural leadership abilities, coupled with a deep empathic sense. They can tell instantly who is having an off day and provide them with the tools they need to lift themselves up. Of course they make incredible teachers and professors, but they could work in any type of career where they are able to pass along their teachings to others. Spiritual author Caroline Myss is a prime example of a teacher, helping others understand the anatomy of their own spirits in a no-BS way.

It's also important for Teachers to know who *wants* the teaching, and not run their mouth imparting lessons to people who have no interest. That can come off as preachy, annoying, or aggressive. As a Teacher myself, I've had to learn to wait for interest. I can easily meet someone and instantly start fixing all their problems and inspiring them to live a new life—even though they never asked for that. We have to understand that we can screw with other people's karmas by telling them things they aren't ready for; part of their journey is to learn it themselves when the time is right and desire is there.

Teachers' high Vata energy makes us especially tapped into the cosmos, allowing us to channel higher Source consciousness. However, the Kapha in us also makes us aware of how to share that knowledge with others. We know that each person must be taught in their own unique way, and we can pick up on the sensibilities of others. Knowing everything doesn't make you a good teacher—it makes you a boring, rambling professor. A good teacher can speak to their students so that the knowledge is received. They know that self-awareness must come from within, and the best way they can educate others is to ask the right questions and remain in a high vibrational state so students can come up with their own answers.

CHAKRAS OF THE TEACHER

Root: Balanced.

Teachers have a strong foundation that ripples out into teaching others. They can teach only from this balanced place.

Sacral: Varies.

A Teacher with a balanced sacral chakra has healthy and strong relationships, whereas one with depleted sacral energy may be disconnected from their sacred sexuality because they are always in teaching mode. One with excess sacral energy may be controlling.

Solar plexus: Balanced.

Teachers have a keen sense of who they are and why they are in service. From this place of balance, they can uplift others who may not know themselves as clearly.

Heart: Balanced.

Teachers feel genuine happiness when they see someone succeed based on their advice, and they feel connected to others, which makes them want to uplift their lives. Teachers think of others as they are learning things, as they're filled with a natural sense of oneness.

Throat: Balanced to high.

The throat chakra gives Teachers the ability to express confusing and complicated topics in a simple way. Their throat chakras are their gift, and what they are meant to use on a daily basis. This is why Teachers love to talk so much and can lose their voice from oversharing.

Third eye: Balanced.

A Teacher has a very open third eye chakra, allowing them to intuitively see how they can be of service to others. They can see possibilities for their students that they may not see for themselves and have a big-picture vision of life. They are highly connected to cosmic and intelligent energy, which channels through them. Omega 3s, such as chia seeds and walnuts (which are literally shaped like a brain!), help keep their minds sharp and brilliant. It's important for them to practice a form of meditation to turn their minds off to prevent anxiety and headaches.

Crown: Varies.

When a Teacher is truly in their flow, they are channeling from Source, whether they are aware of it or not. It's when they give up their power and trust a book rather than their own wisdom that the crown chakra is blocked.

Nurturer

PREDOMINANT DOSHA: KAPHA

The Nurturer is here to care and connect. They find their sense of purpose in nurturing others. They are highly empathic and can feel exactly what a person needs. They are the kind of friend who will invite you over for dinner and make an incredible meal, then truly listen to you talk about everything on your mind. They are natural healers and have an ability to transmit that healing through their love. Simply being in their presence feels restorative.

Nurturers are high in Kapha energy, which makes them patient, good-natured, humorous, loyal, warmhearted, and loving. They don't do drama, and it rarely comes to them. Many Nurturers become coaches, but their coaching style is different from that of the Teacher, who may be more intellectual. The Nurturer is more about emotions and energy. They're here to hold your hand and help you find a way out of your problem, while a pure Teacher is not. The Nurturer doesn't mind someone venting, whereas a Teacher may become annoyed about why that person isn't just taking action!

The Nurturer cares deeply about helping others feel good, especially since their own journey may begin from a lack of self-love. Nurturers often put others before themselves, and it's important for them to practice boundaries. They cannot be everything for everyone and can actually enable people by allowing them to remain in victimhood. A disempowered Nurturer will enable people's dependency on them because it gives them a false sense of power. They know how addictive their love can be for others and may use it as a secret tool to keep people close. They may also fall into codependent relationships, especially with narcissists who demand their full attention.

The Nurturer must learn to use their superpowers wisely, to uplift people without creating that dependency. Nurturers will often say, "People take advantage of my niceness," which really means, "I don't know how to set healthy boundaries with people and I end up overextending myself." The only people who will become upset at your boundaries are those who aren't honoring them. Nurturers often pick up people-pleasing behaviors because they want to satisfy the needs of their caregivers, and subsequently everyone around them. It's crucial for them to create boundaries so they can nurture people fully when their heart is there, and not when it isn't. The most important person Nurturers must nurture are themselves. If your cup is not full, how will you pour into anyone else's?

When shit hits the fan and the Vatas are having panic attacks and the Pittas are livid, Nurturers hold it down, thanks to all that Kapha energy. This is why Nurturers are great with coaching, customer service, human resources, nursing, childbirth, and teaching. Just being around them gives others a sense of calm and ease. Oprah is a prime example of a Kapha Nurturer—she's able to listen empathetically to anyone who sits in the chair beside her and treat them equally, whether it's a major celebrity or an ordinary person with a major problem.

Nurturers' sweet, loving energy lights up the world and makes this human experience easier for everyone. There isn't a person that doesn't love a Nurturer—people around them can feel their compassionate hearts. When they're able to give themselves the love they give everyone else, they're fully able to step up into their power.

CHAKRAS OF THE NURTURER

Root: Balanced to high.
A Nurturer is very connected to the Earth, which is where they get their energy. This root energy is what makes them so stable, even in chaos. However, when root chakra energy is in excess, they become stuck and resistant to change. It's important for them to stay stimulated so they don't feel overly dense and heavy.

Sacral: Balanced to low.
Some Nurturers have strong relationships and are able to give and receive pleasure, while others have difficulty with receiving. They are so used to doing everything for others that they don't know how to surrender. They may not feel sexy, causing them to not want intimacy. They may have such strong motherly qualities that being primal and sexual feels awkward to them, which can manifest as tight hips. It's important for Nurturers to tap into their sensual sides so that they can receive the love they exude to others.

Solar plexus: Balanced to low.
Nurturers can often lose themselves in the pursuit of healing and helping others. After all, their entire identity is entwined with their service to others. Often they don't know who they are when they aren't helping others. It's important for Nurturers to set healthy boundaries to replenish the solar plexus energy that's spent supporting others. Turmeric, ginger, and cumin are beneficial spices for Nurturers to keep them stimulated and detoxified.

Heart: Balanced to high.

Nurturers have a deep sense of love and connection with all those around them. This is what motivates them to serve in the way they do, but they can sometimes become too attached to other people's emotions and end up taking on their energy. As high empaths, it's important for Nurturers to know which feelings are *theirs* and which belong to others. Practice cord-cutting meditations and setting energetic boundaries, surrounding yourself with a shielding light so no energy outside of yours can enter your field.

Third eye: Balanced.

Nurturers are connected with their intuition, which is how they pick up on what others need merely through sense. They are connected to higher power and know that their work is benefiting the lives of others. Sometimes they don't make time for their own spiritual practice, which can make them feel off. It's important for them to continue their own spiritual practice so they can channel that energy to serve others.

Crown: Balanced.

A Nurturer's love is the universal love that is streaming through them. Their care and kindness is an embodiment of Mother Earth's toward humankind.

Visionary

PREDOMINANT DOSHAS: VATA + PITTA

The Visionary is here to be a bridge for the new paradigm. They are especially tapped into universal Source consciousness and spiritual energy, and they're able to express the visions that come through them with the gift of words. They have reincarnated at this time to inspire people to embody their fullest potential. They are changemakers who thrive in leadership positions where the focus is on their message. In Vedic tradition, a Visionary is considered a guru: "the one who leads you from darkness to light." This is not the same as the Teacher, who imparts knowledge. The Visionary is more spiritually focused, whereas the Teacher is more focused on knowledge. However, any true Visionary will ultimately teach you that the only true guru exists within you. Visionaries serve as a reflection of your own spiritual practice, reminding you that you already have the answers within yourself. They won't sulk with you about your latest breakup or that you were fired; they'll lift you up and hold you to the highest level to ask what your experience is teaching you.

A Visionary's art is their speech. They speak enthusiastically, charismatically, and with great spirit. When they talk, people listen. They can rally people around their ideas and shift the energy of the room with their passion. More than their speech, it's their energy that has that impact; when they speak, they're channeling their words from a larger source. Visionaries speak best when they don't write out what they're going to say but just show up and channel. In fact, too much planning will make them nervous, and they won't deliver their most authentic content.

A Visionary's information comes in streams, also known as downloads. They'll be on a walk or in the middle of a conversation and a stream of ideas on how to improve society will suddenly hit them. This is why Visionaries so easily come up with books, programs, movements, courses, lectures, and other offerings that transmit wisdom. They're focused on information rather than physical products and their goal is not money, though it may be a by-product.

A Visionary's life must feel like the unfolding of their words. Visionaries are tapped in with the cosmic web of energy and constantly shift their focus to be in alignment, even if it means completely changing something or launching a new project before the infrastructure is in place. The moment an idea hits, they need to take action.

A Visionary has displayed Visionary ideals since childhood. They are the type of children who want to run for president, end world hunger, petition companies that use child labor, and create a global meditation campaign. If you haven't guessed it yet, I'm #VisionaryAF and it's been evident since I was a wee one. When other kids dressed up as their heroes Marilyn Monroe and Walt Disney, I came in a straight-up robe dressed as Gandhi. Most Visionaries embody the Activist as another archetype because of their deep desire to help humanity. The difference between the pure Visionary and the Activist is that the Visionary uses the power of speech, while the Activist may be more action-oriented. The two work well together and can exist simultaneously within you.

A Visionary is also a natural-born leader; they have an aura that exudes positivity and charisma that attracts others. Although Visionaries are often Teachers, a pure Teacher may feel satisfied teaching a small group, whereas a Visionary desires to share with a global audience. A Teacher may impart a skill not directly related to world change, whereas a Visionary is only interested in what increases planetary vibration. The difference between a Nurturer and a Visionary is that a Nurturer will listen to you cry and vent and sulk with their grounding and soothing Kapha energy, while a Visionary works to bring you higher with their Vata/Pitta action.

Visionaries have a great deal of Vata energy, which makes them extremely idealistic. They say yes to many projects because they're genuinely excited about them, but they often spread themselves too thin, ending up overwhelmed and anxious. Their Vata can make them overly idealistic and underly realistic. Their Pitta will make them take action, even when it's unorganized and not planned out. And their lack of Kapha causes them not to know when to stop, all leading to a great deal of energy expenditure that isn't the most effective. While Visionaries do have a higher threshold than most, they also are energy-sensitive beings who need to turn off and recharge their batteries.

Visionaries can guide others easily, but it's important for them to tune in to when their advice is wanted. Visionaries can come off as preachy to others who don't share the same ideals. They must speak only to those who are ready for the lesson and not give someone more than they can chew.

It's important for Visionaries to remember that the spirit world moves much faster than the physical realm—spirit may be throwing you ideas that you'll be able to manifest in this lifetime, but you don't have to do all of them right now. Focus on bringing one vision to life before you usher in the next. At the same time, if you're being called to action, go for it. Let your intuition guide your way, rather than your fear of not getting everything done. Above all, as a Visionary, your energetic state is of upmost importance. Don't sacrifice your high vibration just to create. Sacred self-care is of ultimate importance because your product is you.

CHAKRAS OF THE VISIONARY

Root: Balanced to low.

There's a certain level of anchoring that's needed to speak ideas into existence and create a movement. Without that grounding, the Visionary wouldn't have resonance. It's their idealistic vision, paired with their grounded sensibility, that makes them so effective. However, a Visionary's work often calls them to be in many places, which can cause them to become ungrounded. It's important for them to focus on their priorities, rather than every idea that comes through.

Sacral: Balanced to low.

A Visionary tends to have a life partner with whom they share their vision. They often work side by side, bringing their movement to life. However, their mission can become the focal point of the relationship and they may not prioritize spending romantic time with each other. It's important for Visionaries to have work-life boundaries. A single Visionary may be so focused on their message that they don't try to meet new people—they feel that impacting the world gives them all the satisfaction they need!

Solar plexus: Balanced to high.

A Visionary has a very keen sense of who they are and what their purpose is. From a young age, they are purpose-driven beings and always want to rally around a cause. They have the confidence to express themselves but aren't overly aggressive. Some Visionaries have not yet fully stepped into their dharmas as global leaders, but as soon as they do, any solar plexus–related imbalances, like IBS (Irritable Bowel Syndrome) and digestive issues, will resolve. Other Visionaries may have a strong idea of how the world should look, based in their own biases, and be judgmental toward other people's opinions.

Heart: Balanced to low.

A Visionary is in touch with the world and people around them, which fuels them with the desire to serve. Unlike the Entrepreneur, the Visionary wants to create a movement rather than a business—the movement just needs a business around it to sustain it. But sometimes, because they are exposed to such difficult matters in life, they can close up to protect themselves. A Visionary has to maintain a healthy distance but must also learn to open their hearts and let people in. If you can't feel the suffering of the world, how will you alleviate it?

Throat: Balanced to high.

A Visionary's strongest chakra is their throat, tied with third eye. They can easily express the wisdom they're channeling through vocal activation and have a natural ability to use words in a way that drives their message home. Unlike the Entertainer, their speeches are meant to plant the seed of a new way of thinking. The Visionary's throat chakra energy becomes excess when they are constantly speaking. A Visionary must know their voice is a gift, and one that must be taken care of.

Third eye: Balanced to high.

A Visionary's third eye is their other strongest chakra, because it is always active when they are in a speaking trance. Any Visionary will tell you that their ideas are not theirs but rather flow through them from a higher power. They experience the downloads that are too poignant to have come from the human mind. A Visionary typically has a spiritual practice because they are in touch with subtle energy. A Visionary must commit to rekindling their connection with Source daily for their highest wisdom to come through. The purity of the guru is of upmost importance in Vedic belief. Blue lotus tea, used by pharaohs in ancient Egypt, is an excellent elixir for Visionaries to open their third eye chakras.

Crown: Balanced.

A Visionary's wisdom doesn't come from them but rather through them, from Source, and this is only possible with an open crown chakra. However, they may sometimes get so stuck in the battle that they lose sight of the universal support available to them. It's important for them to take space away from their audience and peers to tap back into their own channel.

Entrepreneur

PREDOMINANT DOSHA: PITTA

The Entrepreneur is here to address the problems of society through business solutions. They see businesses as more sustainable than ideas or petitions because they have infrastructure, revenue, and a team to keep them going. They aren't going to protest about plastics—they'll create a business that minimizes plastic waste. Entrepreneurs pride themselves on not being complainers, but rather problem solvers.

An Entrepreneur thrives on coming up with solutions that no one else has thought of. They know that time is money and value productivity above anything else. They have a keen sense of their energy levels and pick up practices to keep their focus high, whether it's an adaptogenic drink or jumping jacks before writing. They see the population as a bell curve they must always be ahead of and are thinking about what will happen in the future. There's a kind of "screw the man" attitude in the entrepreneurial community, and you'll find them sharing ways that they hacked the system with great pride. This is why you'll find them in the start-up scene, attending business masterminds, or talking about their latest funnel strategies.

Though the Entrepreneur may come across as nerdy, they're actually the rock stars of today's world. With the rise of online business, everyone wants to be an Entrepreneur. They see these Entrepreneurs taking amazing trips, meeting with influential people, and making more than professionals ever have—all from the comfort of their homes. However, people don't see the struggles. How during that vacation, they had to put out five fires and get on late-night Zoom calls with their team in a different time zone. They see the highlight reel, but they don't see the sweat, blood, and tears behind that one moment. An Entrepreneur often puts their business before everything, often compromising on their self-care, social life, and relationships. However, as an Entrepreneur scales, they realize the value in all of this and it keeps them growing.

With all of that Pitta energy, patience is something Entrepreneurs don't have a lot of. They must learn that not everyone is as motivated about their business as they are. This is why they often feel unsupported: They have the expectation that people are going to care as much as they do, but that seldom is the case. This can cause the Entrepreneur to wear too many hats and take on too many responsibilities, always being "on." It's important for them to build a team they can trust so they can focus on their area of expertise.

The Entrepreneur must learn to accept support and express their needs. Because Entrepreneurs work on their own, it's important to create a support team of other Entrepreneurs in similar industries they can call upon for support and share advice with.

Entrepreneurs also must learn to drop the ideal of perfection. I see so many people who aspire to be Entrepreneurs spending months on the perfect website, perfect logo, perfect business name—and guess what? Nothing ever happens! The truth is, people care about the details way less than you think, and the most important thing is to get it done. You can shift as you evolve, and entrepreneurs are always evolving. Because their mind works so fast, they get bored of routines quickly, and this is why most Entrepreneurs are serial ones. Author Marie Forleo is a prime example of an Entrepreneur, slaying in her business and showing others that everything is figureoutable.

An Entrepreneur's version of work-life balance is different from that of the other archetypes because their work is an extension of who they are. I see a lot of books telling us to put our laptops away at seven and not work on the weekends—but for an Entrepreneur, that sometimes just isn't in alignment with their truth. An Entrepreneur *wants* to work! For example, I used to get annoyed with myself because I'd meditate and drift off into a riveting email I wanted to send out. I'd go to a sound bath and have visions of the gatherings of women I wanted to bring together. *Why can't I just focus on the white light?!* Over time, I came to realize that this wasn't a bad thing—it was a blessing! This is how Source channels through me, providing me with a road map for my dharma. (Entrepreneur is my fourth archetype, after Visionary, Teacher, and Artist.) For these reasons, the Entrepreneur doesn't have the same day-to-day balance as most people but often works in seasons.

I suggest Entrepreneurs align their schedules with the Doshas: a creative Vata season when they're channeling ideas, an action-oriented Pitta season when they're executing those ideas, and a restorative Kapha season when they replenish their batteries. This doesn't mean the seasons need to be equal. Tune in to how you feel. If your work exhausts you, then you need a break. If your work energizes you, keep doing it. Stress only comes when you're doing things you don't want to do for a prolonged period of time. It's up to us to change our state or delegate a task that is not in alignment with our dharma to someone for whom it is.

An Entrepreneur feels bad "quitting" something, especially if they've invested a lot of time or money into it—more so if others have invested time or money as well. But you're not helping anyone if you're not living in alignment with your dharma. An Entrepreneur must know it's OK to pivot. You may be a personal brand, but you are a person before you are a brand, and as a person on a spiritual-growth journey you will be evolving rapidly. Allow yourself to evolve and shed any businesses that no longer serve you as you come into deeper awareness of who you are and how you are here to serve. Trust that you will end up with the business plan your soul came here to fulfill.

CHAKRAS OF THE ENTREPRENEUR

Root: Balanced to low.

An Entrepreneur must have a certain level of grounding to be able to bring ideas to life. A balanced root chakra causes them to execute efficiently, observe what people need, and lead a team. However, their root chakra becomes low when they overextend themselves and don't focus on self-care, exercise, and meditation. An Entrepreneur must remember the business can only grow as much as they do.

Sacral: Balanced to low.

An Entrepreneur struggles with making time for their relationship because their number one love is their business. They can be workaholics. They may not even go out on dates because they'd rather not waste time that could instead be focused on their growth. However, an Entrepreneur only becomes truly on fire when they have the support of a stable relationship behind them. This replenishes them from the soul level and gives them a bigger reason behind their why.

Solar plexus: Balanced to high.

An Entrepreneur has a very keen sense of who they are—so much so that others are investing in their visions. Their solar plexus is their strongest chakra because it fuels them with the power and motivation to create. It is the bridge between taking an idea and transforming it into a tangible result. However, Entrepreneurs often have excess solar plexus energy when they believe they have to do it all alone. As Ayurveda teaches, we don't just digest food but also thoughts, feelings, emotions, and energy. When the Entrepreneur is taking on too much, their digestion suffers on all levels, from their ability to think clearly, to cope with stress, to even physically digest. An Entrepreneur must remember who they are outside of what they have created. It's important for them not to over-caffeinate and to focus on cooling and cleansing foods like leafy greens and herbs.

Heart: Varies.

An Entrepreneur creates their business to solve problems for others, which is an extension of the heart. They have a true desire to help. However, when they're disconnected from their heart, it can become more about the profit than the problem. This is when work becomes an obligation, not an opportunity, and you lose that drive you once had. When your heart is open, you realize that business is just an opportunity to serve.

Throat: Balanced to high.
Entrepreneurs have a strong ability to express what they want to share. Customers and investors can sense their passion, which draws them to support. As an Entrepreneur, you need a certain level of communication skills to effectively share your vision. Entrepreneurs with excess throat chakra energy may talk too much without listening. It's important for them to hear the feedback of their customers and team members.

Third eye: Balanced to high.
Entrepreneurs are receiving information from Source, which is how they receive nuggets of inspiration for their businesses. Though they may not label themselves as intuitives, they are. More and more Entrepreneurs are becoming interested in meditation because they see how much it supports them in their business, which eventually leads to spiritual awareness when they realize money isn't everything. Every Entrepreneur is on a spiritual journey, whether they're aware of it yet or not, and part of their dharma here is to discover the sacred in business.

Crown: Varies.
Some entrepreneurs are highly conscious, practicing meditation, Ayurveda, yoga, breathwork, plant medicine, and other forms of spiritual development, while others care solely about profits and ROI. As an Entrepreneur grows, they realize it's not about the money but about the impact.

Artist

PREDOMINANT DOSHA: VATA

The Artist is put on this Earth to create beauty. They are channels of divine expression through art, song, design, poetry, and/or dance. They are tapped into the beauty of all things, taking in the sights, sounds, tastes, and smells in their surroundings. They need the world around them to be aesthetically pleasing or they feel out of balance. They are very particular about the way they like things and have a signature style to everything they do.

It's important to note that the Artist is not necessarily a professional artist—they're just someone who brings art into everything they do, a messenger of beauty. They'll spend extra time to make sure everything they do is beautiful and become frustrated when people don't share the same attention to detail. An Artist is always reinventing themselves. They tend to have several careers over their lifetimes, or even at the same time. They're the type of people to make the art, come up with the branding, direct and edit the video, design the costume, and even build the set. Everything in their life is curated to reflect their creativity, from their social media feed, to their home, to their wardrobe, to their office.

An Artist often finds words difficult and heady. They want their work to speak for itself, without explanation. They're trying to create something that can stand alone, outside of them, and working with a medium gives them time to think, shape, and form the piece before sharing it with the world. If an Artist does use words, it's usually through poetry or deliberate writing to allow themselves the time and space to edit. They don't think well on their feet or perform well under pressure, especially if there's an audience. (An Entertainer or a Visionary, on the other hand, will thrive in that setting.)

Artists are tastemakers. They don't follow trends but create them—Artists can throw together items from a thrift shop and look like they're walking down a runway. Frida Kahlo is a prime example of an artist creating an iconic style that has lasted decades. An Artist likes to spend a lot of their time by themselves, because they take in so much energy around them. They need extra time to themselves to process that, which then becomes the inspiration for their art. They have a lower need for human interaction than other archetypes and can be hermits.

Artists are intuitive, open-minded, and creative, and bring divine consciousness into the physical plane through their art. They may feel uncomfortable in big groups of people because they're taking in so much information from the world around them. One key difference between the Artist and the other archetypes high in Vata (Teacher and Visionary) is that the Artist's art carries their message, whereas the Visionary's words state their message. The Artist also usually cares less about the "cause" than the Teacher or Visionary, whom the Artist may consider preachy— art, after all, doesn't need a purpose.

It's important for Artists to ground themselves in their physical bodies so as not to become Vata imbalanced, experiencing anxiety or insomnia and feeling scattered or frazzled. This is why those characteristics are so archetypal when we think of the mad artist. If Artists don't ground their energy (Kapha) and connect to the Earth and their physical bodies, they can enter a downward spiral that leads to manic-depressive states and psychotic episodes. If Artists can find a routine that connects them to their body and nature, such as hiking, swimming, or playing a sport, they will be much more balanced and better equipped to continue with their art.

An Artist's greatest issue is sticking to their originality rather than creating something they know will be successful. There may be a demand for them to create something more mainstream, but if it's not true to what they have a passion for, they'll become extremely depressed. Artists do well as creatives, branding specialists, graphic/interior/fashion designers, content creators, writers, photographers, cinematographers, musicians, jewelry makers, painters, and poets.

CHAKRAS OF THE ARTIST

Root: Depleted.

Artists can be very disconnected from their root chakras because their energy is so up in their heads (Vata). For this reason, they need grounding foods like sweet potato, pumpkin, and other root vegetables, and favor warm cooked foods rather than raw foods, smoothies, crackers, and granola bars. They need more routine in their life to anchor their bodies, and a schedule so that their bodies know what time to expect to eat, sleep, exercise, etc. They need to spend time in nature, disconnected from their phones, and to reconnect with their physical body through movement and bodywork.

Sacral: Varies.

Artists' sacral chakra can be balanced, depleted, or in excess. A balanced sacral chakra means that they have a healthy relationship and sex life, depleted means that they have a lack of sensual and sexual energy, and excess means that there's too much. An Artist may have a depleted sacral chakra when they're overly focused on their work. On the other end, they may have excess sacral chakra energy if they are overly dependent on the love and validation of their sexual partners, which is why some artists become serial daters or sex addicts. They can become overly smitten with their muse and lose their grounding. An Artist must balance being in love without losing themselves in it. They must give themselves the validation they seek from others.

Solar plexus: Varies.

Some Artists have a strong sense of who they are, giving them a balanced solar plexus, while others require the validation and praise of others, which means a depleted solar plexus. Other Artists are narcissistic and believe the world runs around them, causing excess solar plexus energy. You'll see all three in the Artist archetype.

Heart: Balanced to low.

Some Artists have balanced heart chakra energy and genuinely want to connect with the people who appreciate them. They have so much gratitude for their fans and go above and beyond to connect with them. Others don't feel a connection with their appreciators, or with anyone. They may want to be left alone and feel frustrated that people are trying to talk to them. You'll see both. An Artist always experiences the oneness of love, however, when they are in their art.

Throat: Balanced to low.

Artists often use their art as a medium for their expression but have a more difficult time explaining it in words. They may not have the explanation as to why they made a decision, or even be able to put into sentences the inspiration they experienced to create.

Third eye: Balanced to excess.

Artists are channeling higher Source consciousness through their third eyes, which is what art is. Their third eyes are open to receive this creativity, and this is the chakra where their energy is strongest. Their intuition allows them to make artistic choices that cannot be explained to the human mind. However, when they aren't equally balanced in their root, they can be extremely in their heads, making them anxious or scattered or suffering from insomnia.

Crown: Balanced.

Artists are connected to the energy waves we receive, which give us the seeds of inspiration that then become our art. Any true artist will tell you the idea wasn't theirs, but rather was embodied through them.

Researcher

PREDOMINANT DOSHA: VATA

A Researcher is here to observe the world, the object of their study, to be analyzed through their lens. They came here to understand the ways of the world on a deep level. They are extremely curious and carry that childlike curiosity with them throughout life. As children, they were always asking "why" and were never satisfied until they got the real answer. A Researcher is not action-oriented, but they prepare the information for other people to take action. They will do the study, which the Entrepreneur, Visionary, Teacher, or Activist acts upon and shares. This is why Researchers make great research analysts, journalists, scientists, investigators, historians, futurists, or doctors, and excel in other data-driven careers.

Researchers are like sponges that can never get enough knowledge. They love sitting for hours and getting nerdy on a subject to thoroughly understand it. However, they often push back their actual careers because they feel like they need to learn more. They may go from one degree to another because it provides them with safety and buys them time to do their favorite thing. But what good is the research unless it is shared? A Researcher must tap into their inner Teacher, Visionary, Activist, or Entrepreneur to get the word out and take action, or pair up with an archetype who can.

Researchers love getting lost in museums, reading every single word about every single display. They are thorough in everything that they do—others may find them OCD, but it's because they're so aware of all of the subtleties of a subject. A Researcher will never speak about a subject they don't know about; if you ask a question they don't know the answer to, they'll tell you they don't know and then come back to you a few days later having done the research. They aren't here to polish their egos. It's like the saying, "The more you know, the more you realize you don't know."

Researchers are integral to society because they're willing to go places that others will not—into the details. Researchers are in the lab curing diseases, creating technology, and shaping the world of tomorrow. They're putting together history's lost puzzle pieces, which helps us understand the world today. The superpower of Researchers is their focus. While others get bored quickly, a Researcher dives in 100 percent. They have no problem spending hours a day for weeks, months, and years to fully understand a subject. They thrive on knowledge—it is their life force. Thus, their motivation is internal. They don't need someone screaming at them to go faster or harder. In fact, Researchers are extremely sensitive to loud sounds, big crowds, and hyperactive energy. The Researcher would rather be left alone with their books.

I do want to clarify that knowledge is not the same as wisdom. Knowledge is acquired, whereas wisdom comes from within. A researcher may gain a lot of knowledge on a particular subject matter but still not be wise in their daily life. The difference between the Researcher and Visionary is that the Researcher is focused on acquiring knowledge, whereas the Visionary is channeling wisdom. The Visionary is more of a spiritual believer, whereas the Researcher is more of a scientific skeptic. This is not to say that you cannot be both: Deepak Chopra is a perfect example of the two archetypes hand in hand. His Researcher background is what caused him to become a doctor and focus his career on providing research for alternative medicine and meditation; his Visionary qualities inspired him to leave his path as a doctor to write about spirituality. Spirit and science are merging more than ever before.

One of the Researcher's strengths is their nonjudgment: They see everything as facts, without forming an opinion about whether they're good or bad. Their ability to maintain neutrality is what makes them excellent judges, mediators, diplomats, and facilitators. Empathy is not their thing; they wouldn't make good therapists or coaches unless they also embody the Nurturer archetype. It's not that they don't feel; they just have a very strong grasp on their emotions and aren't swayed too much by them.

A Researcher is the type of person to take on a hobby and become obsessed with it: They may decide they want to learn Japanese and become fluent in a matter of months, then excel in Japanese calligraphy and poetry. Researchers are also planners who need to know what's going to happen next so they can make sense of the world. They're the people who compile lists of sightseeing, museums, and restaurants for family vacations, then print out a color-coded itinerary for everyone.

Researchers should remember that they can spend a lifetime in preparation, but they will never be totally prepared for every eventuality. Sometimes you just have to take action. Don't use another degree as a way of escaping from the responsibility you have to share your gifts. There are people out there who know far less than you who are changing the world. Allow this to be a message from the universe giving you the permission to begin now.

CHAKRAS OF THE RESEARCHER

Root: Low.
Researchers' energy is so in their heads that they may be disconnected from their physical form and feel awkward in their bodies, which can lead to irregularities and injury. It's important for them to connect with their physical bodies and primal natures, which have been suppressed. Spending time outside, movement, and dance are wonderful practices to awaken their root chakra energy.

Sacral: Low.
Researchers are more in their minds than their bodies. They may not be very interested in sex and pleasure because they're too busy studying. As intelligent as they are, they are often naïve in love and end up with unstable or dominating partners. Because they are so neutral and nonjudgmental, they overlook aspects of a partner that others would have seen as a red flag. It's important for them to be with someone who respects their quest for knowledge, which is often another Researcher.

Solar plexus: Balanced to low.
Some Researchers have a strong sense of who they are and why they're doing the research. However, others can lose themselves

in the research and forget who they are. They may not have any motivation behind their research besides just wanting to learn. It's important for Researchers to take a step back and ask why they want to learn and how it will benefit themselves and others.

Heart: Low.

Researchers are less connected to their emotions. While they are well-versed in matters of the head, they are less so with matters of the heart. It may be difficult for them to name their exact emotion, and they may make generic statements like "I feel fine." Because they're disconnected from their own hearts, they are often disconnected from the emotions of others. Tantra is a wonderful practice to connect Researchers with their heart chakra energy.

Throat: Balanced to low.

While some Researchers have a strong ability to teach their subject matter, others do not. This depends on whether Teacher/Visionary is their other archetype. A Researcher with a balanced throat chakra can share the observations they've made, while one with a depleted throat would not be able to put such complexity into words or have the patience to water it down for others. They move so quickly in their minds, they don't know how to slow things down to make it palatable for others. It's important for them to realize that sometimes a CliffsNotes version is all others need.

Third eye: Varies.

This is a Researcher's most powerful chakra, where all their energy lies. However, this third eye energy is more directed toward the mind rather than its true focus: the intuition. A Researcher is always deciphering things—they think rather than feel. However, they may go with what makes sense on paper rather than what their intuition is telling them. The Researcher truly reaches their power when they can go beyond the "facts" of the 3D and begin to see with their inner eye. Their greatest lesson is to trust their inner voice as much as they do those outside of them.

Crown: Balanced to low.
A Researcher must learn to open up their crown chakra to receive information from universal Source, not just an existing source. There is a reason they are so interested in the research they're drawn to—it's part of their dharma. That feeling of flow you experience when you're deep in your research is kriya and your intuition will guide you to put together the missing pieces of the puzzle.

Entertainer

PREDOMINANT DOSHAS: VATA, PITTA, KAPHA

The Entertainer is here to make you laugh, cry, smile, gasp, ponder, and every emotion in between. Making you feel is their greatest joy. The Entertainer will take something boring and make it novel. Nothing makes them feel more alive than performing, whether it's in front of a crowd or a camera. To them, life itself is a performance, which can sometimes blur the lines between who they truly are and who they are pretending to be.

The Entertainer thrives on being the center of attention. If they're in a dull conversation, they're the one to crack a joke, share a fun fact, or say something totally out of the ordinary. They want to amaze you because it makes them feel amazing, too. They make incredible actors, comedians, hosts, agents, speakers, vloggers, and content creators.

The Entertainer is always trying on roles. They wonder how other people would think, talk, dress, love, and fight. They're constantly observing how people behave and notice their little quirks so they can do a kick-ass impersonation. It fascinates them to be inside the minds of others. Jim Carrey is a prime example of a (very Vata) Entertainer, morphing and shifting into other characters to better understand the human psyche.

If imbalanced, the Entertainer may be unsure of who they are. They play so many roles that it can become confusing to distinguish which is their truth. This is why many professional actors, singers, and comedians struggle with depression and addiction. They feel so much pressure making the world smile that they forget what makes *them* smile. An example is Kapha Entertainer Robin Williams. He was busy making the world laugh but never expressed the deep loneliness he experienced. Entertainers may worry that nobody will like them if they aren't entertaining. This can lead to addiction to numbing substances that make you further forget who you are.

When Entertainers are told to stop playing or shut up as children, they grow up believing it's not safe to be their loud, entertaining selves, and they put their big personalities on a shelf in order to fit in. They feel their gifts are "too much" and they won't be loved if they give them their fullest expression, but the opposite is true. This lifetime is all about reclaiming their voice and owning their gift, knowing they are safe to shine. Chances are they know about their gift but find it hard to admit because it feels too wild and crazy.

Being an Entertainer doesn't mean you have to quit your job and move to Hollywood (unless that's what you want to do!), but it means inviting some of your entertaining qualities back to the table. That can be performing at the company's holiday party, or going to karaoke with your friends, or joining a theater group, or starting a YouTube channel. There are plenty of other Entertainers out there to collaborate with in low-commitment ways.

Entertainers must step into their worthiness. Because our upbringing has taught us that being a professional Entertainer is like winning the lottery, most Entertainers are too afraid to admit to themselves that it really is what they want to do. I call BS! There are so many ways to entertain, and even if the silver screen is your dream, you must honor that vision. Entertainers were born with the passion to fuel them through years of dedication.

Entertainers often blend well with other archetypes, such as Artists and Visionaries. However, they are always easy to distinguish because they place themselves front and center. Artists produce the art, whereas Entertainers *are* the art. And an Entertainer is content just entertaining, whereas a Visionary will always use entertainment to inspire. Both make you feel things, but the purpose behind *why* is different.

Entertainers usually have a deeply spiritual side. Because they are so fascinated by the human character, their understanding goes deeper than the superficial. Wanting to know why humans behave the way they do leads them to the seat of the soul. Comedian Chelsea Handler, known for her crude humor, underwent a spiritual journey that took her to Peru to participate in an Ayahuasca ceremony, which she shared on her show. This is why we see so many actors, musicians, directors, models, and comedians open up about their spiritual practice.

Entertainers can often see both sides of any situation because of their ability to step into different characters. If two friends are arguing, they won't choose a side because they can truly understand both perspectives. Even when an Entertainer is argu-ing with someone, they may change their minds mid-argument and start arguing from a different perspective. Their nature is fluid, and it can be hard for the more rooted archetypes like War-riors to keep up with them.

CHAKRAS OF THE ENTERTAINER

Root: Balanced to low.

An Entertainer with a solid root chakra has a good anchoring in who they are. They have a daily self-care practice, spend time in nature, and know how to disconnect. They know that they are human first, Entertainer second, and don't let their archetype rule them.

However, Entertainers often play so many roles that they can be up in the air, out of their chosen bodies. They must remember to treat their chosen body like a temple. It's important for Enter-tainers to spend time in nature, eat grounding foods like root veg-etables, and stay away from mind-altering substances to ground their energy.

Sacral: Balanced to excess.

Some Entertainers have healthy relationships, while others are serial daters/spouses. An Entertainer is often looking for novelty, which can make them search for it in their dating lives. They want the love to feel like a movie with all its passion, romance, and drama. This can lead to instability and searching for a person to complete them when only they can complete themselves. Some Entertainers become sex addicts because of their need for atten-tion. An Entertainer often has an easier time sharing the depths of their soul with the public than with their partner. An Entertainer must learn to love sincerely and stay committed, even when it no longer feels like a rom-com.

Solar plexus: Varies.

An Entertainer with a balanced solar plexus has a clear knowledge of who they are. An Entertainer with a weak solar plexus is unable to differentiate between who they are and the roles they play. They lose themselves trying to entertain or impress others and end up lonely and depressed. An Entertainer with an overactive solar plexus has placed too much emphasis on their ego. However, this false sense of confidence is easy to see through and crumbles under criticism.

Heart: Balanced to low.

An Entertainer with a balanced heart chakra is connected to the joy they give others through their entertainment. They practice relentlessly because of the positive effect it will have on others. They feel the love of their art and a deep commitment to their service. An Entertainer with a depleted heart chakra is not willing to accept the love others give them because they do not love themselves. They are bitter, sarcastic, and condescending as a way to protect their fragile hearts.

Throat: Balanced to high.

An Entertainer with a balanced throat chakra can deliver their art with ease. They express themselves effectively through speech, song, or comedy, and words slip off their tongue in a relaxed manner. An Entertainer with excess throat chakra energy may react too quickly without thinking. An Entertainer never means to hurt someone, but their quest for always getting the last laugh can put them in tricky situations.

Third eye: Varies.

For an Entertainer to truly be in their power and in expression of their dharma, they must be tapped into their third eye. This grants them the intuition they need to perform the role Source has intended for them to act in this lifetime. When they are listening to the voice of truth, they know exactly how to express their gifts. Though it may be easier to entertain in lower vibrational ways, it is the Entertainer's dharma to figure out the way they were meant to radically express their vibrant truth. When an Entertainer knows their worth, they won't settle for anything less.

Crown: Balanced to low.

When Entertainers open their channel through the crown chakra, they play the role of their life. They will tell you that they have no idea where it came from, but they simply served as a vessel for whatever came through. This moves them from playing a role to belonging in their role on this planet.

Activist

PREDOMINANT DOSHA: PITTA

An Activist is here to bring about social, environmental, or political change. They do not take their time here for granted and are dedicated to leaving the world a better place than they found it. An Activist sees the world as a cohesive being where all people are intertwined. One person's problem is everyone's problem, and they refuse to turn a blind eye to the injustice in the world. Activists are the voice for the voiceless, advocating for protection of the environment, the marginalized, and all living beings. They align their lifestyles with their principles, often becoming plant-based/vegan, eco-friendly, minimalist, and waste-free. They know the impact their choices make, from their clothes to their cars to their meals, and educate themselves and others on being smart consumers.

Activists don't run away from the scary issues of the world; they run toward them. Patriarchy? Mental health? Transgender issues? Let's talk about it. It boils their blood when people avoid real-life issues, preferring to stay in their bubbles. They see it as our obligation as privileged people to discuss these issues and will take every opportunity to be that voice. Activists make excellent lawyers, speakers, nonprofit founders, and influencers.

No matter what career an Activist moves into, social awareness will become a part of it. They will rally their office to nix plastic. They'll style their clients' hair with nontoxic products. They'll teach their yoga class about the importance of spiritual activism. They'll use anything as a platform to share important issues. If an Activist does not have the freedom to bring social justice to their work, they will become aggravated, angry, and stifled.

Activists are very action-oriented, with a ton of Pitta energy. They want to take measures, and yesterday. They aren't willing to sit passively and just be the change, hoping people follow. They will do everything in their power to create it. This drive is not something they should fight—it's an Activist's gift. However, they must learn where to channel that energy. Activists love to debate, but the truth is most debates aren't worth having, especially if they're taking place on the comments section of a social post. If the outcome of your debate will actually create change, then go for it. However, if it's just to prove your point to a defensive stranger on the internet, neither of you will convince the other and there's no point wasting your energy.

Activists see healing the planet as their ultimate spiritual practice. To them, it's about bringing light to the darkest of places. A prime example of this is spiritual teacher and politician Marianne Williamson. At a talk of hers I attended, she spoke about how the spiritual community should be the most politically active. You'll never be totally "healed," but that shouldn't be an excuse to withhold from healing others. She said that the best healing you can have is to put your tears on a shelf, go out there, save the world, and come back and realize how lucky you are. Like a true Activist, Marianne ran for president of the United States in the 2020 Democratic primaries. One of an Activist's greatest gifts is to inspire activism in others. You bet I left Marianne's talk wanting to use my platform for more social activism and then transmitting that inspiration to others. An Activist can make you rethink the world in just one conversation.

While Marianne is both Activist and Visionary, there are differences. The Activist is more focused on the cause, whereas the Visionary is more focused on the message. A pure Activist may prefer to work behind the scenes, on the ground, or on causes that don't have spiritual implications. However, when the two come together, they inspire solutions to real-world problems.

A downside of their passion is that Activists often need to learn the art of sharing information without seeming aggressive or preachy. Being an angry Activist will cause people to get defensive and disassociate. There are tactful ways we can educate someone without making them feel bad. As an Activist myself, I've learned to choose my battles and speak kindly to people who aren't aware of the impact of their choices. No one learns when they feel attacked.

Activists are plugged into a cosmic source of energy that is so much greater than themselves, which gives them relentless energy. As you step into your dharma, you'll notice that you need less rest because there's less energy draining. You're living in kriya with your Dharma Archetypes, which fuels you in ways nothing else can.

If you're an Activist, your dharma is here to bring about global change. Focus on whatever issue makes *your* fire come alive. You don't need to solve all of the world's issues, and you'll be able to get so much more done if you focus on one cause that you make your own.

CHAKRAS OF THE ACTIVIST

Root: Varies.

Activists with a balanced root chakra are grounded in who they are and don't become flustered when someone doesn't agree. They stand firm in their beliefs and don't feel the need to fight everyone who doesn't hold them. An Activist with a depleted root chakra feels unsafe, hence the need to fight. They are constantly defensive and on their guard because they don't feel rooted and secure. Activists with excess root chakra can feel invincible and go overboard, sacrificing their personal safety and also jeopardizing the well-being of others.

Sacral: Balanced to low.

An Activist with a balanced sacral chakra can disassociate from the cause they're fighting to connect with their beloved. They can be a warrior in the battlefield, but come home and be a sweetheart to their partner. They don't take the angst of the workday to their partners and can talk about subject matters that may seem less "important," like their nephew's soccer game or a new movie. An Activist with a depleted sacral chakra has only one mode—superhero. They can't receive pleasure because they feel like they always have to save the world. It's important for Activists to take off their armor for some time and let themselves receive.

Solar plexus: Balanced to high.
An Activist with a balanced solar plexus knows who they are and doesn't need to prove themselves to anyone. They are secure, confident, and anchored in their unique expression. It doesn't ruffle their feathers when someone disagrees with them. An Activist with excess solar plexus energy will feel the need to push their opinions down others' throats. They think only their point of view is correct and get defensive when others don't agree.

Throat: Balanced to high.
An Activist with a balanced throat chakra expresses their opinion with fluidity, precision, and ease. They inspire others to make positive change through their compassionate yet motivational speech. They know how to properly express the importance of activism without coming off as preachy or condescending. An Activist with excess throat chakra energy may go from persuading to yelling. They can be overly aggressive and speak when their opinion was not solicited. This is just their passion spilling out, but they must learn to use language effectively if they really want to get their points across.

Third eye: Balanced to low.
An Activist with an open third eye chakra is a spiritual activist. They are aware of the unseen energies that create our physical reality and advocate things like group meditations, energy healing, forgiveness of those in prison, and teaching yoga to the homeless. They call upon spiritual people to be more involved

in social issues and see our world as an extension of who we are. They understand the connection between all living beings, human and nonhuman, and know that aggression will lead to further aggression. When an Activist opens their third eye, the world truly changes.

Crown: Varies.
An Activist is here to help others, which is an altruistic goal. However, they can sometimes be too focused on the 3D world that they forget the spiritual implications behind it all. An awakened Activist realizes that everything is connected and that raising the consciousness of others is the most important thing we can do for the planet.

Warrior

PREDOMINANT DOSHA: PITTA

The Warriors are here to protect. They have a strong moral compass and a deep desire to safeguard the powerless and give voice to the voiceless. They are strong in their expression and not afraid to be themselves. They know what it's like to be weak, bullied, or taken advantage of, and they never want anyone else to be in that situation. They have strong opinions and a deep sense of what is right or wrong. They have love-me-or-hate-me personalities and aren't here to appease anyone. They are willing to speak up and say what everyone else is thinking, even if it singles them out or alienates others. They are anchored in their own truth. They make excellent fitness professionals, CEOs, motivational speakers, managers, and law enforcement agents.

The Warrior has a primal energy and a deep connection to their physical body. With all that Pitta, they have a lot of energy to burn. They need an intense form of exercise to release the stored-up energy fields in their physical forms. Otherwise, they can become angry, impatient, or aggravated—symptoms of excess Pitta. A Warrior gravitates toward boxing, running, spinning, weight-lifting, and endurance sports. They require a great deal of stimulation and get bored doing nothing. They always need to be figuring something out, which makes them feel like they're using their energy in alignment with who they are. If they aren't solving a puzzle, they don't know what to do with their excess energy and take it out on others.

Warriors were given a great deal of energy because they were meant to find solutions. They often find themselves as entrepreneurs because they can't stand to take directions from others. Regardless, they need a sense of freedom in their position to allow them to make their own decisions. They can't be micromanaged by someone, and a boss may be intimidated by their strength. Warriors are often athletes because of their keen sense of their bodies and drive to win. They are highly competitive and can see the world as "us versus them." They must work hard to overcome seeing all things as black and white, good or bad, right or wrong.

Warriors are highly loyal with strong opinions and will do anything for their friends, but they must understand that their friends may not always be right. They must learn to look at both sides of a situation before making a decision and to not get involved in things that aren't pertinent to them. Warriors often thrive on drama and enjoy being disliked—it makes them feel like they're doing something right. They'd rather be loved by a few than liked by everyone. They give tough love, and that's what people love them for. Nurturers, Researchers, and Teachers often clash with Warriors, whom they find abrasive. Congresswoman Alexandria Ocasio-Cortez is a prime example of a Warrior, fighting fiercely for social justice and reform, even if it means ruffling some feathers.

Warriors have a communal soul and their Pitta energy makes them want to be part of something greater than themselves. They prefer to work with their team in person, rather than online, because it's far more intuitive for them to connect in the physical rather than the ethereal due to their low Vata energy. They often use physical contact in their communication style, such as a pat on the back or a fist bump. Warriors need to share a mission with others and, as good team leaders, rally the troops to keep everyone motivated.

The gift of the Warrior is to motivate others with their Pitta energy. The Warrior thrives on overcoming obstacles, whether it's helping someone drop twenty pounds, invest in a business, or buy something they didn't know they needed. Warriors make incredible salespeople because they speak with such certainty and authority and aren't afraid of hearing "no" over and over. The main obstacle of the Warrior is to overcome polarity. They must know that things exist in shades of gray.

CHAKRAS OF THE WARRIOR

Root: Balanced to high.
Warriors are grounded, primal, and energetic. They are deeply connected to their physical bodies and the Earth. However, sometimes their root chakra energy can be excessive, which makes them competitive, territorial, or angry. Getting into fights is an example of excess root chakra energy.

Sacral: Balanced to high.

Because they are so physical, Warriors tend to be very sexual beings. A balanced Warrior has a life partner they see as their teammate. Together, they are building a family and creating a foundation. Warriors with balanced sacral chakra energy make incredibly devoted and loving partners. However, those with excess can be jealous and possessive. They can also become addicted to sex because of the release it gives them or can use sex to "conquer" someone. It's important for Warriors to find balance in their sacral chakra to become whole.

Solar plexus: Balanced to high.

Warriors have a strong sense of who they are and what it is they want to do in this world. This gives them confidence, courage, and empowerment. However, when this energy is in excess, they can become egotistical and unable to compromise. They may get into too much "us versus them," which makes them compete with the world around them.

Heart: Balanced to low.

A Warrior with a heart is here to protect and serve humankind. They use their strength to lift and support others. However, a Warrior with depleted heart energy just wants to battle. This the kind of person that picks a fight with everyone. A Warrior with a depleted heart chakra can be very dangerous, as the strength is not balanced with love.

Throat: Balanced to low.

Some Warriors have a strong ability to express themselves, while others may be more physical and less verbal. For example, many athletes would never want to give a speech or write a book; however, some do, and they have a powerful message to share.

Third eye: Balanced to low.

Some Warriors have a clear sense of intuition, but most are too grounded in reality to see the in-between. They can move too quickly and don't notice the subtleties. Spirit contradicts itself all the time, which is difficult for Warriors to comprehend. It's important for Warriors to have a meditative practice so they can access more subtle energies.

Crown: Balanced to low.

When a Warrior's crown chakra is open, they are receiving guidance from Source and take action accordingly. When it's closed, they may be fighting for the sake of the fight, without trusting the greater forces at play.

A QUICK RUNDOWN
FOR YOU SKIMMERS

Your Dharma Archetype gives you the unique lens from which you'll view the world and fulfill your dharma. Knowing your Archetype allows you to see what you naturally excel at and the type of work you are meant to do here on this planet.

DHARMA OF EACH ARCHETYPE

Teacher	*To teach and guide*
Nurturer	*To care and connect*
Visionary	*To usher in the new paradigm*
Entrepreneur	*To create profit and impact*
Artist	*To create beauty*
Researcher	*To understand deeply*
Entertainer	*To make people feel*
Activist	*To create a more just world*
Warrior	*To protect and lead*

Which archetypes related to you?

List your archetypes in order.

Who are the people who inspire you? What is their archetype?

7

Finding Your Dharma Blueprint

Now that you have a better understanding of who you are and the archetypes you came on this planet to rock, let's acknowledge something we all face: obstacles. Even though they feel like the universe blocking you, they're actually the universe defining you so you can embody your dharma in a way you couldn't have otherwise. You know those moments when you have no idea how you'll find your way through? *That* is when Source comes through. This is when you become *otherworldly*.

Many people have spoken about these moments, when a voice (often their own) tells them they can no longer live like this and that something needs to fundamentally shift. In the deepest and darkest of places, a light turns on. They remember that they have a purpose. And though they may not have any idea what they're going to do, they take the first step toward their dharma.

Show me someone who hasn't had obstacles and I'll show you a (very boring) unicorn. We have all had some sort of pain or hurdle that we have had to overcome, even those with a privileged life. Why do these painful things happen? It may be karma from past lives. It could be a lesson you signed up for prior to incarnation. We'll never know why for sure. What matters is how you are going to transmute it and turn it into medicine.

The universe never gives you more than you can handle. Whatever you experience, know that you have the strength needed to surmount it. As you evolve, your ceiling becomes your floor. You'll realize the reason the obstacles were given to you was so you can rise above them and see from a higher perspective. The level of pain you were able to overcome will only expand your limits beyond who you once believed you were and strengthen your ability to help others through their pain. If you're going through the mess right now, know that it is shaping your message.

One of my best friends, Tara Mackey, was born to a drug-addicted mother who even did cocaine in the taxi on her way to give birth. Her mother overdosed in front of her when she was six, and she was adopted by her grandparents to grow up on food stamps in the housing projects of Brooklyn. Doctors began prescribing psychiatric medications as a "preventative measure," which went up to fourteen different prescriptions in her teenage body. Her brain chemistry faltered and she became extremely depressed, leading to a failed suicide attempt in her twenties. After hitting rock bottom, her inner guidance came through: Her life had meaning, and she wasn't meant to feel so numb. She began her path of self-improvement, reading books about herbal healing, meditation, and spirituality, which helped her to address her depression and anxiety and begin healing. She began to remember who she *really* was and committed to living her life with purpose. She wrote the book *Cured by Nature*, which is about overcoming depression holistically and sustainably, and now teaches women around the world. As Tara said, "I saw my life two different ways: if I fulfilled my purpose, and if I ignored it. Both paths seemed equally terrifying and difficult. But I knew that the hardest thing would be not trying at all and wondering for the rest of my life what could have been."

The unique obstacles you've gone through were gifted to you for a reason. Only you can share your unique story, from your unique experience. Your depth and understanding of the pain allow you to step further into your passion. There is a reason behind your why, because you've experienced life without it.

Trauma comes from holding on, and healing comes from letting go. When you hold on to something, it's stored in your cellular memory and you keep replaying it. You walk forward with your trauma and it informs every decision you make. When you let go, you create space to rewrite the narrative. Sharing our healing is often the final stage of our process, where we can fully overcome the adversity and create a meaning for it. You don't have to be completely healed to share—sometimes sharing is the alchemy that we need to transmute pain into healing.

Did you suffer from loneliness and deeply need community? That is what you can offer the world. Have you dealt with a health crisis you didn't know if you'd ever see your way through? Why not coach others through theirs? Have you overcome a difficult loss and learned how to heal your broken heart? Others have suffered as you have, and you can share what brought you through the clouds. Did you have a breakdown where you found yourself on your knees crying out for help? Share how you built yourself back up. These are all ways you are transmuting your obstacles into your dharma.

FOLLOW THE RED THREAD

There is a red thread guiding you between every moment, and sometimes you can't trust it until you see how it's been guiding you until now. So let's recognize it together.

Who were you five years ago? What was going on in your life? What were the major themes of that year?

What about four years ago? What shifted? How did the previous year build up to this one? What did you learn that year?

Now think back to three years ago. What was going on then? How can you now see that this wasn't happening to you but rather for you to grow?

Let's return to two years ago. Still feels lifetimes away. What shifted? What did you let go of that year to become who you are today?

Now think back to one year ago. What were the obstacles you were struggling with then? How did you overcome them to bring you to where you are now?

Looking back on the past five years, notice this red thread that ties together all of the events in your life, leading you to this very moment. Notice how you wouldn't be here where you are had even one piece led you elsewhere. When you realize that you are a part of this red thread and everything you've experienced prepared you for this moment, you can similarly trust that you are being guided toward where you are meant to be. Your dharma isn't just one moment; it's the lessons you learn that bring each moment together. All the lessons you've learned in this Earth school have been your unique soul curriculum that you get to embody in a way never seen before.

Let Your Freak Flag Fly

Just as your unique obstacles can lead you to your purpose, so can your quirks. Most of us hide the parts of our stories that feel heavy, embarrassing, or just plain weird. I'm going to let you in on a little secret: The parts of yourself that you're most embarrassed about are where your dharma is. Humans connect to other imperfect humans. We want to see that you've felt the same pain, struggle, and hardships as we did, even if your circumstances are different, because overcoming obstacles is truly universal. When someone sees you've gone through some shit and are still rockin' the light that you are, that is inspiring.

You may think that there's nothing interesting about you, but I'm going to call BS. If we really lean into who we are and what we like at our core—the tribal fusion belly dancing, the tomato ice cream, the unusual sense of humor—we will break out of the pack of people trying to fit in. When you show a side of yourself that no one was expecting, you become memorable.

What is the thing you don't want people to know about you because you're afraid if they do they won't take you seriously? Are you weirdly obsessed with musicals? Do you travel to hula hoop festivals? Do you have a fairy collection? Do you nerd out about Harry Potter? Run with that!

When I began my career spreading the message of Ayurveda, I didn't want anyone to know I loved getting down on the dance floor. I thought that people would only take me seriously as a spiritual teacher if I was wearing an Om scarf, loose white clothing, and mala beads. While I love that look, I had another side— and she loves to twerk. Dharma, dance, and drums is my kinda medicine. Once I slowly started showing those parts of myself, they became the most memorable for my audience. I recently asked them when they saw me at my best and most answers were things like "Your dance videos!" or "When you're DJing!" Of all the things that I do, it's those that are the most out of the box, that I had the most shame around sharing, that are the most significant to my audience and are now an integral part of my work. The very tools that heal me are ones that I share with others, as wild, tribal, and ecstatic as they are. It's time for us all to let go of our domestication and embody our full expression.

We *need* to have our patterns interrupted. It wakes us up from our routines and bring us back into our senses. When we share something about ourselves that's out of the ordinary, we allow others to see that we are multifaceted beings. Wouldn't it be cool to learn yoga from someone who has pink hair and tattoos and plays Led Zeppelin? Wouldn't it be remarkable to practice meditation with a former convict who found his practice in prison? Wouldn't it be relatable to know that your therapist feels anxious going home for the holidays? Humans connect with other humans when we're authentic and vulnerable. When I let you in on a difficult or uncomfortable moment in my life, you see that I'm just a human like you, and it bonds us. You don't need to be perfect to fulfill your dharma—and that's not what people connect to. Your weird quirks, "random" background, and different perspective are what make you one of a kind.

I've been interviewed on hundreds of podcasts, and do you know what I end up talking about more than any other experience? The breakdown moment I shared with you at the beginning of the book. The moment I had the most shame around, that I pushed to the back of my mind because of the sadness it would bring up. *That's* what I end up sharing the most, because that's what people want to know about. They don't want to know how many places you've spoken at, or the accolades and awards you've won. Sure, that's great, but that doesn't make you approachable. They want to see that you've been confused, lost, and broken just like them and were able to get through it. The very things you try to hide are the very things that make you sympathetic.

Vulnerability is a sign of authenticity. As long as you're on this planet, you're in Earth school, learning, growing, and healing. Part of the human experience is to go through waves of total clarity and absolute uncertainty. Owning it and sharing it is an indicator of self-awareness, which is an absolute necessity for living your dharma.

To show you the importance of vulnerability, I'm going to share five uncomfortable truths I *really* don't want you to know about me. I've questioned deleting these from the book a thousand times, but I know I have to take the plunge first for you to trust me on this. So here goes.

1. I'm addicted to my work. I can go on work binges for twelve or more hours a day, forgoing self-care and everything else until I get the job done. I genuinely love what I do, which fuels me, but part of it stems also from my childhood of receiving love from my dad only when I brought home good grades. Having seven planets in Capricorn doesn't help.

2. I'm often numb to the praise I receive and focus more on the criticism. Part of me still wants everyone to like me, which is impossible in today's world, especially when you're putting yourself out there as much as I am.

3. I currently check my social media and email first thing in the morning. I've gone for periods of time without it, but it always comes back. I get anxious not knowing if a message needs my immediate response, then end up watching a random person's Instagram stories.

4. I love future tripping. Especially when I'm meditating. Thinking about what I'm going to do/eat/say/email/write/post next. Me and meditation's relationship status would be "It's complicated." There are times I love it and times that it's the last thing I feel like doing.

5. I get anxiety, overthink, and judge my body. Still. However, now I have the awareness to recognize when it shows up. I call these voices in my head "Overanalyzing Olivia" and "Beatrice" and thank them for their input, but tell them it's not needed.

There, I said it! I'm a spiritual teacher who's addicted to work, still gets hurt by criticism, stresses about the future, and has a monkey mind during meditation. The reason I teach the work that I do is because *I* need it more than anyone else! Does that make you think I'm a fraud? Ignore everything you've read so far, and want to return this book? I hope it helps you see that I'm a human just like you, still learning on this earthly plane.

The only thing that's required for you to live your dharma is to live your truth. It doesn't need your perfection, your degrees, your perfect website. It just needs you to be the most honest version of yourself. If you can see yourself enough to love your flaws, you can see yourself enough to know your truth.

Now, I'd love for you to write down five uncomfortable truths about yourself. These are the things you'd feel most judged, criticized, or shameful about if people knew them. Don't worry, I'm not asking you to publish them in your future book or email them to everyone you know. It'll be just between you and me, I promise.

My Five Uncomfortable Truths

1. ....
2. ....
3. ....
4. ....
5. ....

Whew! How did that feel? Did you notice that the first one maybe scratched at the surface and you got more vulnerable as you went along? If I asked you to write a list of ten, twenty, or a hundred truths, I guarantee you'd still be able to find more. **We suppress aspects of ourselves in fear that we'll be criticized, ostracized, or abandoned if we share them.** These are our *shadow* aspects, the parts we don't want people to see because they're less celebrated, respected, and accepted. They're 100 percent part of you, your unique monsters that you get to slay to reach your highest self. They never fully disappear, but you do get better at handling them. Try sharing these truths with someone and see how light you feel afterward. Share them with me on my Instagram @iamsahararose and read the many others people have shared with me—I'd love to be a witness to your truth!

Uncovering Your Purpose Through Your Chakras

Your dreams are not a coincidence. They chose you as their vessel to bring them to life. The way you usher these dreams into your reality is through the journey of your chakras.

You know that your dharma is your purpose—the big reason you're here. Your chakras are energy centers within the body that keep your mind and body in balance. We speak about chakras a lot in terms of health, but one day as I was walking, a download came through me. Our chakras are more than just wheels of energy within the body. They're the road map with which we usher our dharmas to life.

We don't just come up with an idea and immediately go do it. If we did, we'd be doing pretty much *everything* that came to mind. First, we think about it, visualize it, research it, and decide if it's for us. If it is, we talk about it and write about it. The passion and excitement moves through us as it comes closer and closer to reality. We must then find the courage to take the leap and finally *do* it. However, if we don't find balance around it, it will end up engulfing us. To make it sustainable, we must make the vision larger than ourselves and let it grow its own legs.

This is the system we use to move through the chakras, the ways we channel our energy.

- Crown chakra—The download, receiving the idea

- Third eye chakra—Intuition, thinking about the idea

- Throat chakra—Communication, putting the idea to words

- Heart chakra—Passion, falling in love with the idea

- Solar plexus chakra—Embodiment, taking action to bring the idea to life
- Sacral chakra—Enjoyment, finding the joy of it
- Root chakra—Birthing a movement, making it bigger than yourself

We're all looking for our dharma. And if we use the chakras as our compass, we'll always be guided in the right direction. You can take any passion, put it in the lens of the chakras, and see exactly where you need to focus your attention next.

- You may be in the *crown chakra* phase, where you're still searching for that big idea—this means you should focus on opening yourself up as a vessel to receive.
- You may be in the *third eye chakra* phase, where you're thinking about what the idea will look like—this means you should focus on utilizing your intuition to find absolute clarity.
- You may be in the *throat chakra* phase, where you're trying to find words for your idea and put it to paper—perhaps you are stalled on writing that business proposal, screenplay, or first blog post. This means you should focus on activating your throat chakra.
- Perhaps you're in the *heart chakra* phase—you love the idea but just can't seem to keep the passion for your idea long enough to see it through. Working on your heart chakra will activate that internal fire so you can fire away at your vision.
- You may be in that *solar plexus chakra* phase—hustling away at your dharma, in the midst of the grind. You may

need extra solar plexus energy to keep going and find the courage to take the next step, or you may be ready to allow the next evolvement by taking the sacred pause.

- You may be in the *sacral chakra* phase—you're seeking more pleasure, creativity, and abundance from your work. Activating your sacral chakra will help you find more of these in your overall life, which will channel to your dharma.

- You may be in the *root chakra* phase—you've birthed a movement that is larger than you. Grounding and anchoring will help bring your vision to more people, and open you up for the next dharma that seeks to come through.

Using the chakras as a road map to help you discover and embody your dharma allows you to trust in your journey. The chakras are the compass that points you in the direction of where you need to focus your energy next. **If dharma is your North Star, the chakras are the map points that guide you there.** Each dharma will go through all of the chakras.

You may have one dharma and you consistently cycle through the chakras to further its evolvement, or you may move each of your dharmas through the chakras only once. Either way, bringing any dharma to life will require committing to it enough to bring it through the chakras.

You can also utilize various lifestyle practices to strengthen each chakra, which will flow into how you work with this chakra in your dharma. You may notice that you consistently get stuck in a certain chakra—perhaps it's not receiving the idea (crown), talking yourself out of it (third eye), having difficulty communicating it (throat), feeling detached (heart), becoming overwhelmed by the work (solar plexus), getting burned out (sacral), or missing a community around it (root). The chakras can pinpoint what the issue is, why it's there, and what you can do about it to bring your dharma to life, while also healing the chakra imbalance that affects other areas of your life. **The way you do your dharma is the way you do everything in life.** When you do the work to heal that chakra, it ripples into all facets of your life. Suddenly you'll find you're coming up with more ideas in all areas of your life and bringing them to reality.

Imagine that ideas are floating in the clouds in the highest layer, called the *akasha*. We do not come up with these ideas— they exist, waiting to come to fruition through us. The idea drops upon the crown chakra of those who are a right dharmic fit for it. **This is why you'll never be given an idea that you can't fulfill, because that idea chose you as its vessel.** But that also means ideas are not unique. This is why patents are often filed at the same time in different parts of the country, because two people were gifted the same idea by Source. The idea is ready to come through—it's up to us to catch it and usher it to life. I have found the chakras help us break down this process into smaller steps.

CHAKRAS IN ACTION

- After the idea comes through your crown, you have to think about the idea and through your third eye see if it's right for you and if it's the right time.

- If it is, you then speak about it and shape it into existence through the throat.

- This makes you excited about it through the heart, which fuels the passion to go do it, through the solar plexus.

- From there, the only way you won't go crazy is to find your joy and make it fun through the sacral, so it can become sustainable.
- Only then can it be birthed into a movement through the root chakra, taking its own form.
- You are then free to usher in its new iteration through your crown or move on to birthing another vision.

We have the energies of all seven chakras within us because we are creatrixes, meant to usher universal truths to earthly reality. The journey of our dharma through the chakras is our highest purpose. We are here to be sacred conduits of the divine's messages and bridge the cosmos and the Earth. If we just tune in and take the next step, we will find ourselves bringing Heaven to Earth.

CHAKRA	BALANCED	IMBALANCED	DOSHA	HOW TO ENHANCE IT
Crown	Channeling ideas with ease	Creatively blocked	Vata	Meditation, time in nature, creating space
Third Eye	Thinking with clarity, coming up with creative solutions, believing in yourself	Limiting beliefs, overthinking/analyzing, anxiety, depression, anger	Vata	Meditation, contemplation, reframing your mindset, educating yourself
Throat	Expressing your ideas with clarity	Inability to write or speak your ideas, stuck in your head	Vata	Putting words to paper, dropping perfection and fear of being judged, sharing your idea with others who will offer support

CHAKRA	BALANCED	IMBALANCED	DOSHA	HOW TO ENHANCE IT
Heart	Passion and love for what you do	Not feeling passionate enough to give your all	Pitta	Visualizing all the people you'll serve, making it larger than yourself, getting clear on your why
Solar Plexus	Putting in the work, time, and effort to bringing your dharma to life	Excess: Burnout, work addiction Too little: Not enough commitment and focus	Pitta	Dropping excuses, finding courage, putting one foot in front of the other, not overthinking, taking the leap
Sacral	Finding joy, ease, and fun in your work; receiving abundance, creativity, and pleasure; having balance in other areas of your life such as relationships and self-care	Losing the joy in your project, feeling creatively blocked, lacking pleasure and abundance	Kapha	Remembering what got you excited about it in the first place, making some necessary changes to make it feel more fun for you, taking care of other aspects of your life
Root	Anchoring your ideas into reality, making them larger than yourself, building a community around your mission, taking the sacred pause and creating space for other evolvements to come through	Doing all the work yourself, not sharing your mission with others, inability to create a team/ community around your work	Kapha	Being clear about your why and getting other people behind it, seeking support, creating systems where it can be larger than just you, training and mentoring others

Finding Your Dharma Blueprint

By this point, you know your Dosha and your Dharma Archetype and you may be wondering what to do about it. This is where the Dharma Blueprint comes in. Your Dharma Blueprint informs you of the immediate ways your dharma can manifest. Imagine your archetype as the type of creatrix you are, and the Blueprint as what you're here to cause at this moment. The Blueprint is especially effective for those who are more analytically minded and need a step-by-step process to understand their dharma.

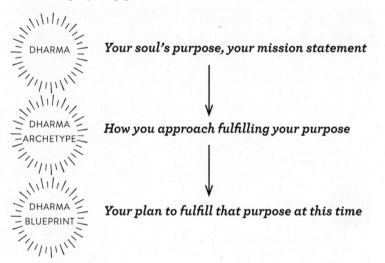

DHARMA — *Your soul's purpose, your mission statement*

DHARMA ARCHETYPE — *How you approach fulfilling your purpose*

DHARMA BLUEPRINT — *Your plan to fulfill that purpose at this time*

When I was on the path of discovering my dharma, I knew I wanted to help people and raise consciousness, but I had no idea how. I knew I loved to write and was extremely creative, entrepreneurial, expressive, and a natural-born teacher. Had I had the terminology then, I'd have known my Dharma Archetypes were a Visionary, Teacher, Activist, Artist, Entrepreneur (in that order). Whenever I left one of these archetypes behind for too long, I would end up feeling unfulfilled. Today, my Blueprint combines these varied sides of me so I feel complete in sharing my gifts. Even if they are not all expressed at the same time, I notice when parts of me are craving a little more attention and I'll bring them out to play. I trust that wherever my Blueprint guides me in the future, it will always be in divine alignment with my Dharma Archetype.

Understanding your Dharma Blueprint will help you figure out how to focus your energy at this time. Though your dharma is eternal, its manifestation will change. Your dharma may be to be a voice for animals—you may do so as an activist, vegan chef, sustainable designer, veterinarian, documentary maker, writer, or something else. **So many people doubt if they even have a purpose because their interests keep shifting, but all that means is that the Blueprint is changing. You're still the same soul creating it.**

Once you know your dharma, you open up your ability to interact with the world in a range of ways. I suggest revisiting your Dharma Blueprint every time you feel stuck and need a shift. Perhaps your superpowers, obstacles, or chosen medium has shifted, and that's why it's no longer in alignment. Once you reevaluate and see what's shifted, you can open up the possibilities to find more fitting ways to engage in your dharma.

Your Dharma Blueprint is where the following meet:

1. Your Dharma Archetype(s)

2. The medium that naturally flows through you

3. What excites you

4. The obstacles you've overcome/helped others overcome

5. Your superpower

LET'S TALK ABOUT EACH ASPECT OF THE DHARMA BLUEPRINT.

YOUR DHARMA ARCHETYPE(S)
Discussed in the previous chapter.

MEDIUM THAT NATURALLY FLOWS THROUGH YOU
We each have powerful means of expression. Our dharma will utilize those that flow most naturally through us. Some of our superpowers are putting pen to paper; others are letting words flow through our lips; others letting colors express our emotions; others producing experiences that are out of this world. We are each artists of our own dharma; our medium is how to bring it to life. Mediums include: writing, speaking, blogging, teaching, designing, analyzing, producing, curating, conversing, coaching, strategizing, painting, singing, photographing, dancing, filming, organizing, visualizing, and formulating.

WHAT EXCITES YOU
What excites you is what gets your vibe goin'! As I've discussed throughout the book, excitement is the key to manifesting your dharma. Without it, you won't have the passion to bring it to life. You must follow the excitement because it is the path of (gluten-free) breadcrumbs leading you to your dharma.

This is the component of your Dharma Blueprint that shifts most often and the reason people kick themselves about not knowing or not having a purpose—what they're excited about keeps evolving. That means the way you are meant to express your dharma has simply changed! It does not mean your dharma has. Your dharma is moving you to a new area. Your work there was done and now it's time for you to take it to the next evolvement.

The transition of your excitement is simply your compass pointing you in another direction on the field that is your dharma. You must give yourself permission to continue evolving for your dharma to unfold.

OBSTACLE YOU'RE SOLVING

The obstacle you're solving is directly related to how you can be of service. For some, it may be direct involvement with people, such as through coaching or teaching. For others, it may be indirect, like creating beautiful art or building a business that makes life easier. No matter what, your dharma is always about being of service. That's why you're here! It just may be on a micro, personal level or a macro, large-scale level, or a transition between the two.

Most often, the obstacle we seek to help others overcome is one we have already faced, because we have the relevant personal experiences and can understand the nuances better than an outsider. You know when you're going through a random personal issue like having a rash or getting a mortgage and suddenly become the expert about it? That's because you are personally invested. Before you know it, you're helping everyone you meet with this problem, and it makes you realize how big an issue it is.

When you have an issue, you make it your mission to solve it. Let's say you suffered from acne growing up. It was mortifying, and you were so embarrassed to be seen in public. So you made it your mission to heal your skin. All your free time was devoted to figuring it out. And you finally did—no dairy, probiotics, a colloidal silver-based face wash, and a three-step skin routine. Victory! You were so overjoyed with excitement that you started helping your sister and a couple of your friends, and decided to put up all your tips on a blog, which led you to develop an online program. People had such great results and wanted to know your favorite products, so you decided to formulate your own. Your Dharma Blueprint became helping people heal acne. But that doesn't mean your overall dharma is healing acne—that's something more overarching, like helping people feel better in their skin.

Having overcome the problem ourselves isn't always required. A doctor hasn't experienced every health condition they're helping others with, but they've studied them extensively, which makes them qualified. In many fields, personal experience is a bonus but not a necessity. In others, such as coaching, it is. I wouldn't take relationship advice from someone who's been single their entire life, or health advice from someone who eats fast food every day. Information does not mean implementation, and people want to seek guidance from those who are walking their talk.

SUPERPOWERS

Your superpower is your how. It's the secret sauce you bring to everything you do. It's the tool underneath your cape that turns ordinary into magic. You often know your superpower because people compliment you on how you do something in ways no others can. If people keep telling you that "You're so good with details" or "You keep such a beautiful home," then that's part of your superpower. Superpowers come in many

shapes and forms, and we all have many of them. For exam-
ple, one of my superpowers is bringing spiritual wisdom to
the world in a way that's fun and relatable. What are yours?

Your Dharma Blueprint combines these categories, allowing
you to see how your dharma can manifest in real life.

1. Your archetype is who you are.

2. The medium that flows through you is how Source moves
   through you.

3. What excites you is your sacred messenger.

4. The obstacles you've overcome are the best ways you can
   serve.

5. Your superpower is the Source-given talent you were
   meant to share.

Together, this creates your Dharma Blueprint, giving you the
road map to where you are going. Then it takes an ounce of intuition and following the signs for your dharma to unfold.

To give you some examples of how Dharma Blueprints work,
I've listed some figures you may recognize so you can clearly see
how they are doing their dharma.

Dharma Blueprint Examples

DEEPAK CHOPRA

Dharma Archetype: Teacher, Researcher, Visionary,
Entrepreneur

What medium flows naturally through him: Writing and teaching

What excites him: Meditation, spirituality, science, non-duality

What obstacle has he overcome or helped others overcome? Not having a strong spiritual foundation, mental stillness, or inner peace

What's his superpower? His ability to create book after book proving spirituality with scientific research

Deepak Chopra is doin' his dharma!

LILLY SINGH

Dharma Archetype: Entertainer, Artist

What medium flows naturally through her: Comedy, making skits

What excites her: Bringing humor to common issues people experience

What obstacle has she overcome or helped others overcome? Being misunderstood as a bisexual woman of color

What's her superpower? Her humor, drive, and work ethic

Lilly Singh is doin' her dharma!

AMMA THE HUGGING SAINT

Dharma Archetype: Nurturer

What medium flows naturally through her: Love, devotion, meditation

What excites her: Healing the world through physical touch and motherly love

What obstacle has she overcome or helped others overcome? Being outcast by her family for having healing abilities and spiritual gifts

What's her superpower? Embodying the divine feminine through her healing hugs

Amma is doin' her dharma!

GRETA THUNBERG

Dharma Archetype: Activist, Visionary

What medium flows naturally through her: Speaking

What excites her: Protecting our environment and preventing climate change

What obstacle has she overcome or helped others overcome? Not being listened to as a young woman, Asperger's syndrome

What's her superpower? Her ability to call the masses to action to come together and protect our environment

Greta Thunberg is doin' her dharma!

This may seem obvious to you because these people are clearly successful, but let's see how going through this process can reveal anyone's Dharma Blueprint!

Lynna was an intern of mine who took my Discover Your Dharma course, then discovered her dharma (and quit the internship, but I'm happy for her!). Here's what it looked like for her.

LYNNA

Dharma Archetype: Artist

What medium flows naturally through her: Design, graphics

What excites her: Conscious consumerism, beautiful branding

What obstacle has she overcome or helped others overcome? Feeling lost, not knowing her purpose

What's her superpower? Her ability to translate her visions into beautiful art

Her Dharma Blueprint: Create her own conscious shop with beautifully branded products

Now let's have you guess what this person's Dharma Blueprint may be.

LIBBY

Dharma Archetype: Nurturer, entrepreneur

What medium flows naturally through her: Teaching

What excites her: Self-care

What obstacle has she overcome or helped others overcome? Adrenal fatigue, burnout

What's her superpower? Her ability to bring her soft, loving persona to hard-minded entrepreneurs

Now what do you think her Blueprint is? How do you think she can use her skills to share? What ideas do you have for her? I'll tell you what she wound up doing at the end of the chapter!

Highest Self Meditation for Your Blueprint

Prayer is how we speak to the divine; meditation is how we listen. Most of us are dying to know our dharma but we aren't listening to the whispers nudging us in that direction. When you ask the right questions, you get the right answers. What I've downloaded is that each archetype must meditate on their own unique affirmation to allow their dharma to reveal itself. Meditate on this affirmation in the morning, in the evening, when you're on walks, when you're about to sleep. Keep stating this affirmation until the sentence completes itself. Whatever comes up, as weird or far-fetched as it may seem, listen to it. It is the bridge to your dharma. If you are a combination of archetypes, practice the different affirmations at different times.

Take a seat, close your eyes, come to your breath. Notice how you're breathing, any sensation in your body. Acknowledge any sounds around you, any thoughts that are lingering in your mind.

Inhale as you count to the number seven. Hold for four breaths. And exhale for seven breaths. Ground down into your root chakra, feeling your connection to the energy of the Earth. Allow your breath to deepen and your body to soften. Repeat this for several minutes, until your mind and body feel calm.

Now, according to your predominant archetype(s), allow your intuition to complete the sentence(s).

- Teacher: I am here to teach . . .

- Nurturer: I am here to support . . .

- Visionary: I am here to share . . .

- Entrepreneur: I am here to make . . .

- Artist: I am here to create . . .

- Researcher: I am here to understand . . .

- Entertainer: I am here to make people feel . . .

- Activist: I am here to help . . .

- Warrior: I am here to protect . . .

Continue to faintly state this affirmation, allowing the sacred pause. You may instantly complete the sentence, or you may hear nothing. It may go on for paragraphs and even change every time you come back to this meditation. Trust that you are doing the work and digging deeper into your soul with each practice.

It may start like a simple idea. You may be inspired to teach about juicing, which leads to creating a social media account, which leads to an eCourse, which leads to a full-fledged juice bar and delivery service. You may be inspired to help pregnant women, which leads to getting trained as a doula, which leads to your own birthing center. We are never able to see the endgame, nor do we need to. All we need to do is ask the right questions and follow what unfolds, sun-being.

By the way—Libby launched a self-care course for burned-out entrepreneurs and is now considering becoming a functional medicine doctor after her own doctor helped her heal her health issues by digging deep into the underlying causes of her ailments.

A QUICK RUNDOWN
FOR YOU SKIMMERS

The obstacles you've gone through have been guiding you along a red thread that has always been leading you toward your dharma. Each obstacle unlocks a soul lesson you are meant to overcome for more total embodiment. All it takes is being radically real about yourself. Sharing five uncomfortable truths about yourself may be the most bad-ass thing you do (and more memorable than anything on your résumé). Remember—people connect to people, not perfectly curated social feeds.

The chakras not only bring you balance, but are guiding you toward your dharma. They are the birthing process to bring universal truths to earthly reality, through a step-by-step process. Your dharma is your purpose, your Dharma Archetype is how you approach fulfilling this purpose, and your Dharma Blueprint is the expression of this purpose.

YOUR DHARMA BLUEPRINT CONSISTS OF:

- Your Dharma Archetype
- The medium that naturally flows through you
- What excites you
- What obstacles you've overcome/helped others overcome
- Your superpower

Use your Dharma Blueprint to unlock the code of what you're meant to do next.

8

Taking Action Requires Courage

Y ou've always been ready for your dharma—you were literally born for it—and at the same time, you're never going
to be totally ready for it. Don't you love a good duality?
Ah, the joys of being human.

The part of you who has always been ready wants to just
freaking do it. You feel like you've been waiting your entire life
for this moment. It feels so close, like you can just reach out and
grab it. But the part of you that is never ready is like, "That looks
like a lot of work, responsibility, and time, and I just don't have
that right now!" That part of you is entrenched in the everyday
tasks, hurdles, and responsibilities that plague you. It's not totally
wrong. But it's not totally right either. Both sides are important
and balance each other out.

You'll never be 100 percent ready. So the important thing is
to learn when you're ready *enough*. You learn *through* the fear.
If you feel like you're totally ready for everything you are doing,
you aren't pushing yourself enough. Everyone is nervous, but the
secret of successful people is that they do it anyway.

Your quest to discover your dharma prepares you for embodying it. The more you stall around being ready, the more resistance you create. The only way to become ready is to choose that you are.

We cannot embody our dharmas if we do not trust our dharmas. Honestly, most of us still hold on to an idea of what our dharma is supposed to look like. When dharma comes knocking on our door, we just don't listen. It comes in the form of opportunities showing up without you even really trying. It comes in people being amazed by things you think aren't anything extra. Life has a plan for us way bigger than our conscious mind can even begin to fathom.

If we can just learn to follow the intuitive guidance that comes to us from Source, then we don't need to question anymore. It becomes really freaking obvious. What is that thing people keep asking you for help with? What is the advice you keep giving to people? What seems to come really naturally to you that other people struggle with? What can you do with your metaphorical eyes closed that takes a lot of practice for others?

Obstacles Keeping You from Your Dharma

The universe throws you obstacles when it's calling you to rise.

I polled my audience to learn the biggest obstacles keeping them from discovering and embodying their dharma. When I read through their answers, I felt like I was talking to one person—the same person I was when I was searching for my dharma. They all had the same doubts, fears, hesitations, worries, and patterns! I want to share them with you to show you that you're not alone.

That those negative beliefs you have aren't unique to you—and so, they're not part of you. They are borrowed from outside sources. It's time for that old paradigm to end.

Fear of not being good enough

Second-guessing yourself

Time management

Familial conditioning (your family or partner doesn't understand)

Societal pressures (worrying what other people will think)

Lack of courage

Unable to connect to intuition

Losing yourself doing what you thought you should

Choosing fear over love

All the old mantras you subconsciously gave yourself

When you were at your lowest

Deprogramming and reprogramming your beliefs

Fear-based thinking

Lack mentality (not enough money, market too saturated)

Overwhelm (not knowing where to begin, too many ideas)

Anxiety

Jealousy

Feeling "weird"

Distractions

Impatience

Now that we know those fears are there, let's talk about them. I'm going to dive into the top four obstacles people face when discovering their dharma and show you how to overcome them.

1. CONFUSION

The number one reason people aren't living their dharma is that they believe they're confused. More than ever, we're exposed to different timelines: Someone is living their best life as a travel blogger in Bali, another as a mom with the cutest four-year-old, and another as an entrepreneur with two seven-figure businesses. They all sound great and look pretty epic on social media, so we have no idea what we're meant to do ourselves.

Back in the day, there weren't that many options available to us. As a woman, you either became a stay-at-home mom or a nurse or a teacher. As a man, you could follow in your pop's footsteps or go under your neighbor's wing. Now there are millions of possibilities, with millions more being created every day. People are Tantric life coaches and holistic interior designers. It can be pretty confusing to figure out what you want to do—and what if you choose wrong?

The thing is, there's really no such thing as confusion. Often we feel "confused" because we haven't fully grasped what our intuition is telling us. There is one truth, and that is eternal. Confusion is just the blurriness that happens when you aren't listening to it. The answers are already inside of you—your fears just aren't letting you hear them.

We act like "confusion" is a bad thing when it's actually a great thing. **What we experience as confusion is really a process of evaluating our own truth.** Confusion is a higher vibration than apathy. It's a sign you're on the path of discovering your dharma. You can't gain clarity without first going through confusion. We often push away uncertainty, feeling guilty for not knowing exactly what we are doing, when those are actually the most pivotal moments of our lives. Confusion is necessary before clarity because it's in that process that you find your truth.

Ride the waves of uncertainty. They're the only path to clear waters.

If you feel confused by all the contradicting advice you receive, I'm going to give you the exact prescription you need. It's not the one you want, but it's the one that's going to change everything: Go on an advice detox. For one month, I want you to not ask anyone for advice on anything. Not your mom, your bestie, your spouse, and especially not the internet. This is going to be most effective when you feel the most "confused," because that's when you're reevaluating your truth and need your clearest thinking without it being affected by the thoughts, fears, and experiences of others. Sure, there are times when advice is beneficial. It's when you don't know the difference between your opinions and others' that you need to stop, because that's when you're saying, "Someone else knows what's best for me better than I do."

Asking others for advice without listening to yourself is giving up your power to someone else who isn't you. If you constantly call someone else to ask for advice on every move in your life, I suggest you reclaim your power and ask your highest self for the answers instead. This is not to say you should never ask anybody's advice ever again. Allow in advice when you are anchored enough in your own truth to not let that change the trajectory of your life. Take every piece of advice with a grain of pink Himalayan salt and check in with your internal compass first.

You know those people who instantly shoot down your ideas and come up with a list of reasons they won't work? Don't share your ideas with them, especially when you're still in the Vata stage of figuring out your dharma. Because your dharma still hasn't been set in stone, one of these conversations may prevent you from ever bringing it to life. Their intentions, insecurities, or fears aren't yours to take on. Treat your dharma like a precious newborn and only show it to those who can hold space for it.

Some people may be so triggered by you following your dharma that they can't help but try to knock you down. You may not even be able to share your dharma with some of the people closest to you. It can feel hard to withhold such a tremendous aspect of your life, but if you leave every conversation with them feeling defeated, learn that lesson. Once you've found the strength to do it and it's already in motion, *then* you can share, if you so desire. But while it's still that precious newborn, you need to keep it safe.

When you do feel you are at a place where your inner GPS is strong and even a hater can't knock you down, you are ready to open yourself up to advice, but be selective about who you seek advice from. Seek advice from someone who has done similar things to what you envision. If you want to be a writer, sign up for a writers' workshop. If you are thinking about life-coaching, talk to some life coaches! It can be more challenging to ask someone for advice who's actually doing the thing—they're probably busy, you don't know them, you feel awkward reaching out. However, only they can give you an answer because they've gone through the process and can shed light on areas you may not be even looking at. Even they don't have all the answers, as no two dharmas are the same. **Treat advice like a buffet—take what resonates with you and leave the rest on the table.**

Some people may keep trying to give you advice even when you aren't asking for it, like your parents. They believe that this is the way they can show you love. Often their entire relationship dynamic has been based on the parent/adviser, child/advisee dynamic and they feel jobless without it. This is a boundary you're going to have to set, both internally and externally. I suggest telling that parent that you're going on an advice detox, and as much as you appreciate how much they care, you're working on listening to yourself more clearly. You'll let them know when the doors are open for advice again. They may not take this well, but it's important you speak this truth and mark this boundary clearly. Let them know that the best way they can show their love is to allow you to navigate this time in your life on your own.

Another reason people can be "confused" is because they haven't tried it yet! I've had students ask me, "Am I supposed to figure out my dharma by trying a million things and seeing what sticks? That sounds like it'll take forever!" That fear of taking too long keeps them from taking action at all. The truth is, yes, you're going to have to try a couple of things before you figure it out. No one gets it on the first try, and even if they do, it's going to evolve. But that's the fun part. You get to experience life in so many different ways and see what fits for you. More than ever, we're embodying many different careers in a short amount of time, because it's never too late! Life spans are longer than ever before, so even if you're starting a new career at fifty, you still have a good number of years ahead of you. It's not game over, it's just halftime! And as any sports fan knows, halftimes are a chance to reevaluate, reassess, and fine-tune the strategy for the next half.

We've always known about the midlife crisis, but now so many of us are experiencing the quarter-life "crisis," which is actually an *awakening*. We've realized far earlier in our lives that we don't need to keep up with the Joneses in order to be happy—they're all depressed. We aren't willing to sacrifice our lives for a paycheck. This doesn't make us selfish; it makes us self-aware.

Often we say we're confused when we're really afraid of what other people will think. If the reason you aren't discovering your dharma begins with the words "I don't want them to think," you aren't being true to yourself. Some people are going to label you crazy. That's a sign that you are breaking the norms and doing something right. If you aren't startling people at least a little bit, then you're playing by the old rules, which is not your dharma. **You were meant to create something that has never existed before, and that's going to require you to be OK with not everyone liking you.** If you're confused, you're on track. That means you're asking the right questions. Most people never even get to the point of being confused because they accept their circumstances and never shoot for more.

2. NOT ENOUGH-NESS

The number two reason people aren't embodying their dharma is *themselves*. Do you recognize what that means? No one is stopping you but *you*. "Not enough-ness" is the disease that plagues the conscious world. I guarantee that there are way too many humble people reading this book who have no idea how fucking magical they are. They doubt themselves and second-guess themselves when people with half their self-awareness are just *doing* it!

Feeling like you're not enough is actually the first step toward self-actualization. You can admit you don't know it all. You know you have work to do. That shows a lot of humility and introspection, which is a great thing. However, it becomes a bad thing when it stops you. According to a Science of People survey, the number one reason people don't like others is that they find them fake. We don't even like people who are too polished! So why do we feel like we have to have three PhDs and $10 million in the bank just to be enough?

You are enough. The fact that you are breathing makes you enough. That you are taking the time to read this book shows that you are committed to making yourself a better person. You've done more inner work than most of the population already. Goddess, you are so fucking conscious and self-aware! You have so much wisdom to share. You have so much personal (and past-life) experience to tap into. Think of anyone you see as someone who's absolutely made it in their dharma. I guarantee they're not bowling full strikes every single time. Imagine Oprah saying that she's not thin enough to help people, Einstein saying he's not good-looking enough to be listened to, or Malala Yousafzai saying she's not old enough to make a difference in the world. Can you imagine if they had let those thoughts hold them back from sharing their gifts?

We all have our own shit, and that's what makes us relatable. My personal worry was, "I'm not old enough to write a book on Ayurveda. No one will listen to me. No one even cares about Ayurveda." And those limiting beliefs were echoed by more than thirty publishers who rejected me and dozens of literary agents who never even responded to my query. I had every reason to believe that was true, until I decided it wasn't. The fact that I'm a millennial writing about a 5,000-year-old health system *is* what makes it unique. People who resonate with my modern, fun approach will listen to me, and my enthusiasm will make them care about Ayurveda. The very things I thought made me not enough are exactly what made me who I am.

So ask yourself:

Where do you feel like you are not enough?
How could that be an advantage?
What can you tell yourself to remind yourself that you are enough?

3. NOT KNOWING WHERE TO START

Maybe we took part in too many board games as children, but it's like we're waiting for someone to pull out the instructions and tell us exactly how to play. But wouldn't it suck if your only career options came from a stack of cards? Think about it: We get to play life by our own rules and start wherever we want. You want to start by quitting your job? Hell yeah! You want to start by going to school? Right on! You want to start at an internship? Go for it! This is not a marathon where we're all sprinting on the same course. Discovering your dharma is like Alice going through Wonderland. It's trippy as fuck and sometimes it doesn't make sense. But when you look back, you realize it's all connected.

The truth is, the place you are meant to start is right here, right now. Whether you have been aware of it or not, you have been in your awakening process. The fact that you're reading this now tells me that. Every moment until now has been preparing you for this one.

You gotta trust divine timing. You needed specific soul lessons, certain experiences, the meeting or letting go of particular people to discover your dharma. It is all perfectly unfolding. **We cannot ask the sun why she didn't rise sooner. You too will rise in your own divine time.**

Instead of beating yourself up over why you didn't know sooner, give gratitude to the knowing you have now. Had you not traveled down that path, you wouldn't be on this one. Everything had to unfold exactly as it did to give you the awareness you have now. Would you take back any of it? If even one experience was not gifted to you, you wouldn't be here, on this journey of discovering your dharma. **Nothing happens *to* you, but it happens *for* you to evolve.** More than that, it happens *through* you as the creatrix of your reality. You've been gathering the pieces; now it's time for you to step up into your highest self. This begins by remembering your sacred power and evolves into taking action as you gather momentum, propelling you toward truth and expansion.

4. NOT ENOUGH TIME

Often we wait for the perfect moment to start. Amazing how your schedule for next month always looks so clear, until it's next month, right? And then it's somehow even busier than the previous one. Do you find yourself saying, "Things are really crazy but next week they'll clear up" week after week? That's just called life, honey.

The truth is, the only gatekeeper that can make space for your dharma is you. Life is always going to throw you more plans, so you're the one who has to decide which are worth it. Sometimes we get pissed off with others. "Why do they keep inviting me to things? Don't they know I'm busy?" But it's really our responsibility to use discernment. You have to create that space to dive into your own dharma.

You don't need *completely* empty days on the calendar to make progress on your dharma. Never underestimate what you can do in an hour if you use it wisely. Make a date with your highest self. Put it on your calendar, clean up the room, pour a nice drank (adaptogen elixir, please!), take away any distractions, put that phone on airplane mode and delete social media apps (or even leave it in your car if the addiction is that bad). Write out an agenda for your meeting and honor it. Would you start washing your dishes or checking your email while a guest is over? Then why would you do that for your highest self, the queen of all possibilities? For example, your agenda could be, "Do market research on comparative businesses in my desired space," or "Apply for at least five jobs that feel in alignment with my dharma," or "Write first five pages of book." Again, even if you feel like a total Vata who isn't good with time management or organization, doing this will change everything for you. (And it's the exact Pitta you need!)

Now that the meeting agenda is set, close your eyes and drop in for a quick meditation (even just a minute) to tap into your highest self. Set your intention. Call on your highest self to merge with you and implant you with the divine creations that you were meant to embody in this lifetime. Envision white light flowing through your crown chakra (top of your head), allowing Source to seamlessly flow through you.

Use an affirmation that feels right to you, such as:

I am a vessel for the wisdom that moves through me.
I invite my dharma to come through.
I receive the wisdom that seeks to embody itself through me.
I am a conduit for the ideas that have chosen me to usher them to life.
May I be of service, ushering in the new paradigm.

It's important to offer up your session to the benefit of humanity because things will best manifest when they are in service of the whole. **Manifestation only works when it is of service to the greater good of all**. The universe is benevolent and wants what is best for the whole. If you can tie your dharma to something bigger than yourself, it will flow right through you.

Now it's time to get to #werk! Allow yourself to create as the information moves through you. If you are being guided to write about a certain thing or research something else, trust it. Practice letting your intuition guide you, rather than your mind. Ride the channel of inspiration until it runs dry. When you feel yourself hitting a wall, this is your invitation to sink into the Kapha and surrender for a little while until the Vata spark comes through again, ushering you into the Pitta.

Holding a ceremonial container for your dharma is of upmost importance because it's the conversation we're always having. If something urgent comes up that's not related to your dharma, write it down to be addressed after your date, rather than rushing to it then. Your dharma isn't gonna hang around if you keep watching people's Instagram stories while she's there. You gotta show her some love!

Our Words Are Our Wands

The way that we speak to ourselves matters more than any other conversation we'll have. For many of us, it's often a toxic relationship filled with doubts and undercutting remarks. We all know about the power of positive affirmations but let's be real: What are the affirmations you're giving yourself on a daily basis? "I'm so dumb," "I'm so overwhelmed," "I'm never going to figure it out." These words become the record we walk through life with. If you want to do your dharma, you've got to talk to yourself like a person who already is. "I'm learning so much every day," "I can feel myself evolving," and "Every day is bringing me closer to my dharma" is a much better soundtrack.

We live in a society that's so afraid of coming off as arrogant that we've created a culture of self-deprecation. Being proud of yourself does not make you conceited—it makes you confident.

We skim over our accomplishments and focus on our failures, mostly to get the approval of others. Have you ever had a conversation that was a competition over who's busier, who's more stressed, who's fatter, essentially whose life sucks more? Why do we feel we can only bond and connect with others when we put ourselves down? It doesn't make someone more relatable; it just creates a culture of insecurity.

Imagine if we rejected that negativity and lifted each other up instead. When someone complains about how stressed they are, ask them what went well for them that week. By choosing not to engage with them at that self-deprecating level, you can raise them up.

Similarly, our internal dialogue can be high vibe AF.

What do you wish others would say to you?

....

....

What do you wish you could be seen and recognized for?

....

....

What are the things you do that you'd like to be thanked for?

....

....

Instead of waiting for someone to notice, begin recognizing yourself! Tell yourself the exact words you are so hungry for: "Sahara, I am so proud of you for all that you do. I love how you channel wisdom through you with such grace and fluidity. I love how you take action on your ideas and share them with the world. I love your balance of feminine and masculine energies. You are helping so many people that you aren't even aware of." **Now, what's yours?** Here's an example.

"Jolene, I love what a committed mother you are and how you always find the best in any situation. I love how great a listener you are and how you can help others through any situation you're going through. I admire your patience, strength, and resilience."

Now it's your turn. Write down the words you wish someone else would say to you, then say them to yourself. That was the person your soul really needed to hear it from all along.

We put so much pressure on the outside world to speak us words of approval when really what we are searching for is approval within. **When you begin feeding yourself the words you've been craving from others, you begin healing yourself and paving the path toward your dharma**. If you've been waiting for someone to say "I'm proud of you," you may have said yes to high-ranking opportunities that looked glamorous on the outside but actually left you unfulfilled. If you've been waiting for someone to say, "You are enough," you may find yourself in situations where people doubt your worthiness. We have to address our underlying conditioning that makes us choose the actions we've taken thus far. Nothing is coincidental, so we have to be very careful that we're living with intentionality.

The Pitta Stage

We can think, plan, and talk about our dharma all day, but nothing's going to move the needle until we begin doing it. As discussed earlier, many of us stay in the Vata phase. We love thinking about our lofty visions for our dharma—such as writing a bestselling book, producing an award-winning documentary, running a thriving non-profit, or launching a successful product line—to the point that we end up forever adding elements to our dharma list without actually getting anything done. Staying in the Vata phase is a sure way of never taking your dharma off the ground. You have to take messy, wavering, uncertain action, because that action is what is going to give you clarity on all the answers your soul is seeking. You don't learn to throw darts by thinking about it. You learn by throwing them until you hit a bull's-eye. So start writing pages of your novel or short stories even if you scrap all of them after the first year. Or start experimenting with your skin-care line and packaging until you have one product to take to the farmers market.

We often fear taking action on our dharmas because of the "risk." "What if I try and don't make it?" The truth is, there's no risk in following your dharma, because you are 100 percent guaranteed to make it as long as you stay committed to your truth. It may not be what you thought it was when you initially set off on the journey, but it will be your highest point of resonance. Along the way, you learn lessons that prepare you for the next iteration of who you were meant to be. When people say the odds of finding your purpose are like winning the lottery, they're living in fear. You were chosen to live your dharma—the question is, are you going to step up to being in your highest service?

Dharma is a process. You may not get a deal on your first book, but that shouldn't stop you from writing. You may not succeed in your first year of business, but that means you know what to shift for the second. **"Failure" is just feedback as you refine your dharma.** Can you remember your first time driving on a highway?

You were probably scared shitless and had to give yourself a pep talk and stay in the right lane the whole time because everyone seemed to be going so fast. But now you barely even think about it. This can only happen through repeated practice. So why do we expect to instantly crush our dharma the first time around? It's the progress that makes us flow with it.

Most of us don't even give ourselves a fair chance because we are so afraid of failure. This fear cripples us and keeps us from going for what we want. **The truth is, the only way you *won't* fulfill your dharma is if you don't go for it. Your fear of failure is guaranteeing your failure.** A practice that really helped me overcome this is picturing the worst-case scenario. Sounds grim, but my fear was so crippling that I had to face head-on what would happen if I failed. I had all these doubts and fears that seemed so woven together that I couldn't unravel them. So I went there and asked: "What's the worst thing that could happen?" And I kept asking, "And then what?" Until I realized that the worst thing that could happen is actually the best thing that could happen.

Here's an abbreviated version of how mine went:

If I commit to my dharma, what is the worst thing that can happen?
My parents will disown me and never talk to me again.

And then what?
I'll feel horrible that I let them down.

And then what?
Well, I'll probably get over it and realize that it was never my job to make them happy. My priority needs to be making myself happy.

And then what?

 *I'll become free and not live for other people's
 expectations.*

And then what?

 I won't feel guilty about following my dharma anymore.

And then what?

 I can fully step into my power unapologetically.

Sometimes the worst thing that can happen to you is the best
thing that can happen for you.

Now it's your turn to do the practice.

*If you commit to your dharma or embarking on the journey of
discovering it, what is the worst thing that can happen to you?*

....

....

And then what?

....

....

And then what?

....

....

And then what?

....

....

Keep going until you find the blessing. There's an opportunity for rebirth in every perceived failure. The Goddess Kali Ma, who embodies transformation, is a divine reminder of this. She comes forth when you feel like your entire life is up in flames and everything seems to be hitting the fan. She does this so that you can let go of all that is not serving you and reclaim your truth. Sometimes you need to burn the house to the ground to build a new one from scratch. **When you let go of everything you are not, you can step into who you truly are.** It is only in the great void, the cosmic womb, that all possibility is created. We so deeply fear the space between the inhale and exhale that we live in hyperventilation, without understanding that it is only when we pause that we truly breathe.

A friend of mine was working to become a lawyer, but every time she studied for the bar, her health deteriorated. Her body was crying out to her—but she'd just graduated from law school! When she failed the bar for the second time, she finally confronted the truth—that she actually didn't truly want to be a lawyer. Her education in law school serves her in different ways, but her truth was to be a freelance editor—and now she can write her own contracts! Perhaps one day she'll edit a book about law or maybe her soul just needed that experience, but right now, all she can do is honor the truth of where she's at right now and let Kali Ma burn that house down. The only failure is not learning from experience.

Dharma Is Not a Spectator Sport

Imagine if I woke up every day at 6 a.m. to sit and watch a yoga class. I don't miss a day. I watch them downward dog and backbend and even handstand. Would that make me a yogi? Not really! If I tried to go into crow pose or a headstand after years of observing but no practice, I'd topple over pretty quickly. I'll only become a yogi by practicing yoga myself. Dharma is the same thing. You'll only learn by getting yourself onto that mat and into practice.

When I was on my journey of discovering my dharma, I created a clothing line made of recycled sari materials called Saraswati Couture to support victims of sexual trafficking in India. I so deeply believed in the cause, and it fueled me with excitement. However, after two years of vending at dozens of festivals and everything that comes with trying to build a clothing line, I knew in my heart that it was not my dharma. I wanted to serve through sharing my knowledge rather than products. Today I'm able to help those same women in a way that is more aligned with my gifts.

Any dharma will require some effort, but it's up to you to decide if it's the type of effort you actually want to make. The only way you can know is if you get yourself in the game. Most of our speculations about what a career actually entails are completely inaccurate. Want to know what Hollywood actors spend most of their time doing? Sitting around on set. Want to know how most performing artists spend their time? In transportation. If there's something you have a fantasy about, see what the day-to-day is actually like. Would you want to spend your time going to meetings all day? That's what that CEO actually does. Would you want to spend your time alone writing on deadline? That's what the writer does. We have to be real with ourselves about what pain points we're willing to deal with, because every dharma is going to have them. I could never be an actress because I hate sitting around and waiting, but a friend of mine loves it and uses the time for meditation. You may hate the pressure of writing on deadline, but I enjoy it because it forces me to channel my best work without lollygagging.

Think about a career you're fantasizing about.

What would be its related dharma (mission statement)?

....

....

What's so awesome about it?

....

....

What are the shittiest components of it? Let's be real.

....

....

What would that require from someone who is doing it? What qualities would they have?

....

....

Does this line up with your qualities?

....

....

EXAMPLES:

Career: Naturopathic doctor

What's awesome about it is: I get to heal people with alternative modalities.

What's shitty about it is: I have to go to naturopathic medicine school for four years, do a two-year internship, and then take another couple of years to build my business.

What it would require: Someone who's extremely patient, able to sustain the long game, loves to study, and doesn't need income for the next six to eight years.

This does not line up with my qualities because I need to make an income ASAP, I don't like to study, and I'm too impatient to wait that long.

Career: Life coach

What's awesome about it is: I get to motivate people to become the best version of themselves.

What's shitty about it is: I have to get certified in life coaching and do a lot of inner work, it will take me a while to build my business, I won't have a determined income, and I risk financial insecurity.

What it would require: Someone who is a self-aware and an entrepreneurial risk taker.

This does line up with my qualities because I am extremely passionate about doing the inner work myself and I know I won't fail because no one can help others the way that I can!

Now, I could give you all the personality quizzes, knowledge, and information your little brain can grasp to consciously figure out your dharma. But it really comes only through taking action. When you move toward your dharma, you feel an air of release, a brisk wind of motivation, a crystalline sense of your direction. Suddenly, your dharma doesn't feel like a distant mirage. It's right there, before you, within arm's reach. You can't think your way into dharma. You have to walk the path, one step at a time.

What is one piece of action I could take right now to bring me closer to my dharma?

_____

_____

What have I learned through experience that isn't what I want?

_____

_____

How did it show me more of what I do want?

_____

_____

Who out there is teaching something that may be related to my dharma?

_____

_____

What books/programs/classes/conferences can I attend that could educate me toward my dharma?

_____

_____

Dharma Embodiment Practice

Our reality is based on our energetic state. We can agree that our energetic state creates our thoughts and our thoughts create our reality. Therefore, our energetic state creates our reality. If you want to feel aligned, stand up straight. If you want to feel alive, sweat. If you want to feel open, stretch. However our body feels, our mind will respond. Embodiment is the practice of using the body's wisdom to guide us from "body up" instead of from "top down" cognition.

Dance has been my greatest tool toward dharma embodiment, and I believe it will soon be as popular a healing modality as yoga. For thousands of years, we have been dancing, and only in recent times have we thought it's limited to choreography. **Dance is not about a performance—it's an expression of your soul through the medium of your body.** We spend so much time in our minds trying to "figure" things out. Guess what? The mind will never figure it out. The nature of the mind is to loop around in circles. You must leave the mind and enter the body to come back home into your heart. We hold on to so much tension somatically in our Earth suits, and dance helps us release the accumulated tension so we can come back into our true Goddess nature. As you let go of the body and mind, you enter the soul.

I've developed my Dharma Embodiment Practice to put your body in the right state to receive your dharma. This practice awakens each of your chakras to clear any blocks and tap into their full potential. It puts you in alignment with your purpose, power, play, and pleasure.

Do this practice first thing in the morning to set you on the right path of your dharma. Practice again when you're working on your dharma to open up the channels to receive. You will be amazed by what comes through.

This practice can take anywhere from five to twenty minutes, depending on how long you have. The longer you have, the more deeply you'll anchor into it, but even a couple minutes can do a world of wonder.

DHARMA EMBODIMENT PRACTICE

STEP 1.

Shake your arms, legs, and hips, allowing yourself to let loose. Say "ahhhh" as you release any tension you're holding. Ground your feet onto Earth and let her take in all that is no longer serving you. Imagine yourself literally shaking off the stress and limiting beliefs.

STEP 2.

After several minutes, stop shaking and begin circling your hips. Circles cultivate feminine energy in the body (which both men and women have), creating more ease and fluidity. Allow yourself to feel your curves and then bring the circular motions to all parts of your body—chest, shoulders, wrists, neck.

STEP 3.

Create waves with your spine, as if you're body rolling. This awakens the kundalini and moves energy up your body. Try body rolling up and down, letting your neck loose.

STEP 4.

Place your hands over your heart and pop your chest up and down. This activates the heart chakra energy. Practice exhaling "hoo" with each pop.

STEP 5.

Come into stillness with hands on your heart, and feel the love energy you've created. Your heart has its own brain—tune in to it.

STEP 6.

With your eyes still closed, place your hands out with palms up and declare "I receive" either mentally or out loud. Exhale and soften your breath.

STEP 7.

Allow yourself to receive any wisdom and transmission of energetic healing that comes through.

This practice is a game changer. I promise you—after giving this practice a try, you will feel different and manifest at a much higher frequency. Many people experience enormous shifts after just one practice, which grow exponentially as you continue to practice. Notice the opportunities that show up and ideas that come through just from you inviting this energy in. It's magic, I swear. And the best part is, you always have access to it.

Tapping for Your Dharma

Sometimes you feel out of focus and need a reboot to get you on track. Tapping is one of my favorite techniques for reprogramming the subconscious mind and aligning it with higher thoughts that better serve your growth. Tapping, also known as Emotional

Freedom Technique (EFT), is a form of psychological acupressure based on the same energy meridians used in traditional acupuncture to treat physical and mental issues for over five thousand years, but using the tapping of your fingers rather than needles. When you tap your fingertips on specific meridians while you think about your issue and voice positive affirmations, you clear the "short-circuit" emotional block from your body's bioenergy system, allowing you to overcome any emotional issue.

When tapping, it's important to address what you're actually feeling in this moment (confused, frustrated, unsure), and then speak the positive affirmations to overcome them. It doesn't matter whether you believe the positive affirmations yet or not, just say them. It's all going into your subconscious one way or another, and it's best to speak the statements with feeling and emphasis, as if you truly believe them. It's also best to say them out loud, but if you're in a public setting, saying them under your breath or silently is fine. We want to think about our current issue first, before going into the positive affirmations, so that the energy disruptions related to it arise. We then want to overcome them with positive affirmations. Here is one I wrote specifically for your dharma. Feel free to change the words to explain further how you are feeling.

To begin EFT, simply take the fingers of one hand and begin tapping solidly and repeatedly on the areas below, while repeating the affirmations below out loud or under your breath, with emotion.

MAKING DHARMA EASY TAPPING
Top of the head: *Though things may be difficult now and I'm feeling uncertain*
Eyebrows: *I completely love and accept myself.*

Side of eye: *I am willing to overcome obstacles in order to expand.*

Under the eye: *The more I commit to my dharma*

Under the nose: *The more ease I experience.*

Chin: *Ease is a natural result of being who I am.*

Collarbone: *My dharma is meant to feel easy.*

Under the arm: *I am in alignment with my dharma.*

Repeat three times.

Take a deep breath and sigh it out.

You are now set up to live your dharma from a place of ease, fluidity, and understanding.

DISTRACTION TAPPING

Top of the head: *Even though I try to distract myself and keep checking my phone*

Eyebrow: *I completely love and accept myself.*

Side of eye: *I will no longer be distracted from my dharma.*

Under the eye: *Every time I want to pick up my phone or do something else*

Under the nose: *I will shift my focus back to my dharma.*

Chin: *I will come back to it with even more energy, focus, and passion.*

Collarbone: *And have a breakthrough unlike any other I've had before.*

Under the arm: *I am in alignment with my dharma!*

CONFUSION TAPPING

Top of the head: *Even though I sometimes feel confused and overwhelmed*

Eyebrow: *I completely love and accept myself.*

Side of eye: *I invite my brain to relax.*

Under the eye: *I know my dharma is within me.*

Under the nose: *I'm awake and aware of the signs guiding me to it.*

Chin: *I know I'm actually not confused but am exploring options.*

Collarbone: *And these options will guide me to my truth.*

Under the arm: *I am in alignment with my dharma!*

ANXIETY TAPPING

Top of the head: *Even though I have SO many thoughts and am worried I'll never find my dharma*

Eyebrow: *I completely love and accept myself.*

Side of eye: *I know these thoughts are guiding me somewhere and are guiding me toward my dharma.*

Under the eye: *Nothing is wrong with me and I am exactly where I need to be.*

Under the nose: *I will use my thoughts toward my creativity.*

Chin: *I have nothing to worry about and am completely on track.*

Collarbone: *I am grounded and anchored in my truth.*

Under the arm: *I am in alignment with my dharma!*

First Steps to Take Action Toward Your Dharma

You may be thinking, "I'd be game to take action . . . if I knew what action would even look like!" This is just an illusion. On a deeper level, you already know—it's just a matter of finding the courage and confidence to admit it to yourself. **Confidence is simply a result of doing things you're proud of,** like sending a cold email or approaching a stranger at a networking event or writing the first draft of your book proposal.

Here are some examples of easy ways that you can take action toward your dharma:

- Dive deeper with one of my Discover Your Dharma courses.

- Join a biweekly Dharma Support Circle where you share your progress and cheer each other on. (We have them and plenty of resources available for you in my membership community, Rose Gold Goddesses).

- Diversify your social circle and spend time with other people following their dharma, even if it's not similar to your own. Their energy will rub off on you and you'll learn from their habits.

- Get coached by someone who inspires you.

- Set weekly goals. Want to write a book? Make it your goal to write one chapter a week.

- Make it a priority. What will your life look like a year from now if you take consistent daily action? What will it look like if you don't?

HOW TO HAVE MORE FIRE (PITTA)

Dharma requires passion, which is ruled by Pitta, the fiery Dosha that gets shit done. We all have Pitta energy, though it's naturally more pronounced in some. To execute our dharmas, we need to let the Pitta come out to play.

Here are some Pitta-enhancing practices:

- Up your intake of Pitta-increasing ingredients such as ginger, cumin, cayenne, and turmeric. Anything that's hot increases your Pitta. (Just do so in moderation so as not to overdo your Pitta either!)

- Sweat. Pitta is activated through vigorous exercise. When you don't know if you can push any further, Pitta energy takes you up a level. When you're able to overcome the mental blocks when you work out, they become much easier to overcome in the rest of your life.

- Schedule your Pitta-related tasks during a time naturally strong with Pitta energy: 10 a.m. to 2 p.m. When the sun is highest in the sky, our Pittas are activated. For you night owls, Pitta also increases between 10 p.m. and 2 a.m., which may be your prime time.

- Shamanic shaking. This is an ancient practice of shaking your body by jumping and wiggling all of your limbs to get your blood flowing, oxygen circulating, and Pitta firing.

- Time blocking. Schedule your days by task, rather than by hour. List everything you need to do on your calendar and assign it to a time. Make three lists: your biggest priorities, like working on a long-term project; typical workday tasks, like answering emails and taking phone calls; and non-work activities, like yoga and making dinner. Schedule your most difficult tasks at your most productive times (think 10 a.m.–2 p.m.) and your less important tasks in your less productive times. If you're a morning person, work on those big priority tasks in the morning, then answer your emails and do your dishes at night, or vice versa. Also be sure to schedule in your self-care, workouts, and walks. If it isn't in the calendar, it isn't going to happen. I also recommend scheduling several hours weekly for creative time, where you can just work on whatever ideas are bubbling up.

- Break up a big project into steps. Work backward from the desired outcome through all of the steps necessary to get there.

- Create your own mood. Often we'll wait to feel "inspired" before taking action, when inspiration really comes *through* taking action. Put on some motivating music that gets your body moving, like hip-hop and reggaeton. (I share my Pitta-boosting playlists in Rose Gold Goddesses!)

You don't have to do it all right now. The biggest question I get about doing your dharma is: "What if I have thirty different things I want to do?" My answer is first, I feel you. I want to do all of the things, too! Our generation has become very Vata-minded, in that we have our head in fifty places at once. Being multi-passionate is awesome, but being all over the place is not. We want to walk that line with awareness. What's going to move you further toward your goal, making one percent progress on twenty things or twenty percent on one thing?

When you have one project off the ground, you have more space and awareness to take on another one. Here's a good question to help you decide which to focus on now: If this was your last year on the planet, which would you want to leave the world with? Which experience is more pressing for you? Start there.

A QUICK RUNDOWN
FOR YOU SKIMMERS

You're never going to be one-hundo ready. You just have to figure out when you're ready enough. You learn through the fear. Confused AF? Perfect! Confusion is the process of evaluating your truth, aka you're on the right track. Go on an advice detox and use this time to ask your highest self what's up. Your intuition may feel like a pen pal you haven't written back to in a while but trust me, she's excited to fill you in.

You don't have to know where to start. Just start and that will show you where to go next. The universe responds with corrective action. You learn through the feedback. So get goin', goddess! The only gatekeeper to your dharma is you. The only way through confusion is action. Tapping, meditating, and mindset shifts will illuminate the path so you won't keep driving around in circles.

9

Putting in the #Werk

Your dharma is going to take effort, and there's no way around that. But "the #werk" carries a different vibration than "work." What comes up when you hear the word *#werk*? For me, I instantly want to snap my fingers, pop 'n' lock, and gear up for a dance-off. I'm enthusiastic, confident, and feel like a total boss.

This is the energy we want to feel around our dharma. Think Missy Elliot coming out on a unicorn to cheer you on with a private performance of "Work It." It's uplifting, inspiring, motivating and *fun*! #Werk allows us to rewrite the stories of hardship and struggle and reminds us that it is a freaking blessing to be able to do our dharma. You say "HELL YEAH" to the hours. "HELL YEAH" to the emails. "HELL YEAH" to the customer service. "HELL YEAH" to the growing pains, because that means you're GROWING! And that makes every ounce of #werk worth it.

We're pleasure-seeking beings, and when we find pleasure within the effort, we put in the #werk. The thing is, you don't have to trick yourself to make it fun. When you realize that you're living your soul purpose, you're ecstatic. That in itself is enough to get you off-your-socks excited about doin' the damn dharma. **There is nothing more pleasurable than living a life of alignment.**

As a society, we've become so afraid of putting in the #werk. We keep looking for a shortcut: the least amount of effort for the most reward. I mean, does anyone else figure out ways to make it look like you're working when your boss walks by so that you can actually be on social media the whole day? School taught us how to be really good at cramming for tests to get the grades needed to get by, but how many of us actually recall the dates of the Oregon Trail or how to calculate the area of a pentagon? We don't remember because we didn't give a fuck. It wasn't applicable to us. But now we've carried that approach into the rest of our lives, when it actually does matter and you're the only one who's going to benefit. There's no one looking over your shoulder to make sure you did the dharma #werk. That's on you, boo. We need to drop the attitude that we're going to get anywhere without at least a little bit of effort.

Imagine doing exactly what you do best, being acknowledged and celebrated for who you are, and knowing that each and every day you live your life to your maximum potential. And you'll still have tons more energy to go around!

Are you someone who does the bare minimum to get by?

....

....

What is your relationship with work?

....

....

What does #werk feel like for you?

....

....

When has your work felt like #werk?

....

....

What can you do to make your work feel like #werk?

....

....

Imagine your dharma is your boo. You have an incredible, twin flame relationship, and you know there's no one else in the world out there for you. However, the relationship doesn't feel as easy as it did in the early years. You have some things you'd like to say that have been bothering you, but you really don't feel like having that difficult conversation. Do you call it quits and wish each other farewell, or suck it up and have that difficult conversation to fix the relationship?

Most people call it quits. When things feel a little uncomfortable, they dip. And this is why they never experience true dharma. You and your dharma are going to hit some rough patches, but don't let her go. Hold on tighter, put your ego aside, and see where you can show up and recommit yourself to making you and your dharma work. (Here's a hint: If it's not worth it, it's not your dharma.)

Remember, the only way you can fail is if you give up. You are guaranteed to live your dharma if you just commit to it. It's easier to pay attention to the negative noise, because angry people are always louder than happy people. And after all, people living their dharmas are ... well, busy living their dharmas, so you don't hear from them as much as you do from your uncle who tried to go on tour with his band and failed. But the reason he's hurt is that he quit. If he'd stayed the course of his truth, his tour still might have failed—but he might have ended up as a music manager, producer, or drum teacher, something that still utilized his gifts.

A helpful guide is that true love is always expansive, whereas fear is always contractive. If a person really wants the best for you, they'll encourage you. People often want to keep you where you are because it's close to them. Pay attention to the motives for their advice. This is why it's usually important for us to go on an advice detox while figuring out our dharmas. Each person will come with a new perspective and it can throw you off track. Believe in your dharma enough that when you share it with others, even if they try to tamp it down, it's already anchored.

Who do you get your advice from?

....

....

Are they living their dharmas?

....

....

Do they encourage you to live yours?

....

....

Are they giving advice in hopes that you'll remain close to them?

....

....

There's a misconception that one day you'll suddenly stop feeling afraid, and that's when you'll finally take action. You have to move through the fear as your voice is shaking, show up when all you want to do is leave, and step up when you really want to step out. **Doing your dharma is a result of taking action through the fear.** Indeed, there would be no such thing as courage without fear. And eventually, through taking consistent action, you won't feel the fear anymore. The butterflies when you speak begin to melt away, the awkwardness you feel when meeting new people dissolves, the pit in your stomach when you show your work softens. But this only happens when you keep showing up, fears and all. Our fears lead us to our freedom.

Path of Least versus Most Resistance

Sometimes to follow the path of least resistance, you have to follow the path of most resistance. In a perfect world, we all would have *always* been supported to make decisions in alignment with our dharmas. However, most of us don't live in that world. We've gotten so off course with our dharmas that we've set ourselves up in a web of structures that do not serve us. To come back to the path of least resistance, we have to take the path we are most resistant to because it's so far from where we are today. Sometimes what appears to be the path of least resistance keeps you stuck, accepting conditions that are not serving your highest evolvement. The perceived path of least resistance can feel comfortable but that comfort is an illusion, *maya*. It's just accepting conditions that you are afraid to change.

Imagine you are on a beach, trying to get to the open water. You have to swim through currents that will push you back to shore. Only when you've learned to duck and become stronger will you make it out to the open water, and that's where your dharma is. It isn't always easy—everything you've feared will show up, and it may feel like the path of least resistance to give up and let the waves wash you back to the familiar beach where you once were and pretend you don't even want to make it out to the open water anyway. But that's lying to yourself. When you commit to swimming against the current, moving against the limiting beliefs and societal conditioning, you make it to your dharma.

The point is not to always choose the most difficult option either, but to follow what brings you the most expansion. If you know getting through this period of resistance will lead you to inevitable expansion, take it on. You will get through it and it'll be worth every bump on the road. But if you are just choosing resistance for the sake of martyrdom, then it isn't serving you. Take on the path of most resistance when it leads to the path of least resistance. Even an airplane needs to meet resistance in order to take off.

- What am I resisting?
- Why am I resisting it?
- Where would it lead me?
- Do I want to go there?

As you step into your dharma and your fears show up, approach them with gratitude. As you see each obstacle as a divine lesson in your unique schooling, you realize what a gift it is. You've already overcome so much—what's going to stop you now?

Fill in the following prompts, either out loud or in a journal.

Ten things I'm grateful for today are...

I am grateful that my parents taught me...

I am grateful that my childhood taught me...

I am grateful that my partner/former partner taught me...

I am grateful that I am me because...

I am grateful for my current situation because...

I am grateful to be reading this book because...

I wouldn't be here if it wasn't for ...

....

....

I know the universe is supporting my dharma because ...

....

....

After you've written your answers, consider the following:

What came up for you when answering those prompts?

....

....

What surprised you?

....

....

What did you feel resistance toward?

....

....

What did you overcome?

....

....

How did it make you feel easier?

....

....

Make gratitude your daily practice. It's the first thing I do every morning and also part of my *Yogic Path Reflective Journal*, along with my other morning/evening practices. Check in with yourself regularly, and update the answers to these questions. It will help remind you to open your heart as you continue on your dharmic journey.

Stop Pushing Away the Good-ish

Want to know the real reason most people never embody their dharma? It's because they push it away. We get distracted, procrastinate, and give everything else a higher priority than the one thing that actually matters—our life purpose.

Imagine I brought you a present and said, "You're absolutely going to LOVE what is inside. It's the gift of your DREAMS that you didn't even know you've been waiting for your entire life!" Would you procrastinate about opening it up? Decide to scroll through your phone instead? Put it on your to-do list and never end up actually opening it? Heavens no, you'd be opening that shit up as soon as I handed it to you. Then why do we procrastinate our dharma, which IS that gift? To receive it, all we have to do is remain present.

When we are afraid of the responsibility and power we will hold when we finally step into our dharma, we shy away from it. We make every excuse about why we don't have the time and it's never going to happen for us, just because we aren't choosing it to happen to us. **What would your life be like if you fully stepped into your light?** What changes would you have to make? What people would you have to drop? What habits would you have to let go of? Stepping into your dharma is real, and it's going to make everything that is not 100 percent true fall off like leaves of a tree. Sometimes we are too attached to our dead leaves to allow the new ones to sprout.

Do you believe you are worthy of living a life you designed? Do you believe it is possible for you to embody your purpose? Do you believe that you have everything it takes to be an example of what's possible for others? Because it is the absolute truth. You just haven't seen it. If you just realized your power, you'd be kicking yourself over why you ever doubted it even for a moment.

Have you ever been working on a project that really lights you up and suddenly when you're at the brink of something, it's too much? You have to go to the refrigerator or check your phone or just do anything that takes you away from the task? That's your ego blocking you from your dharma. The ego likes to know where it's going. It's always been in the driver's seat of your life. So when you step into something that is so much larger than you, your dharma, your ego minimizes you to keep you on the predictable path. At that moment you are expanding your energetic body, which is why it feels so intense, and your ego can't handle the enormity of who you are becoming. This is why it triggers you to step away, create separation, and subsequently shrink yourself from the magnitude of your soul.

It's in those very moments when all you want to do is step away, but instead you choose to remain present in the expansion of yourself, that the path to your dharma is paved. Your ego may feel overwhelmed because it's seeing a glimpse of how expansive your soul is. You only know a sliver of who you are. When you let your soul take the steering wheel and drive you to the depths of your consciousness, you end up in places your ego could have never expected.

Listening to your soul means awakening to your power. We cannot go on undermining our gifts and strengths any longer. The time has come for us to remember who we are and fulfill our soul missions. Nothing is coincidental, and you are never assigned something your soul cannot handle. The goal is not to have it easy; it's to make it easy. As you ascend, things will fall into flow. But it's only through aligned action that this can manifest. When you remember the truth of who you are, you wake up to why you're here. This moment of absolute clarity is the most blissful feeling in the world. You realize everything makes sense. You are divine. Your dharma is divine. It clears any lingering beliefs and reminds you that truth is the only thing that matters and the only reason we are here. If we can commit to truth, we will become our highest evolvements.

All I can tell you is to trust this shit. Not trusting it only got you this far. What would the road look like if you trusted that the only key to embodying your most blissful self is to believe that you can? **Believe in your damn self. Trust your damn self. Love your damn self. Take action for your damn self.** Because in doing that, you serve the needs of humanity. So how do you do it? It's a decision. It's deciding that I'm going to live this life for myself, which simultaneously raises the vibration of the planet. It's reclaiming the sovereignty you've given up.

You don't need to go on a silent retreat or be blessed by a monk to have a major life transformation. Sometimes it's the shittiest moments that wake you up. You'll awaken whenever you allow yourself to. It will seem like the floodgates have opened and everything that's not in total alignment with your truth will be swept away. It can feel like you're about to vomit from how much you're spinning, and your head's hitting the wall. But that's how you prepare yourself for what is to come—living your dharma.

You realize truth, which makes you realize the truth of who you are. And then anything less will feel like you're being stuffed into a mason jar. You were meant to take up space, use your voice, share your gifts. Anything less is a disservice to humanity.

Remember, your soul is ancient—it may not know about the latest in digital marketing (that shit you're going to have to google in this lifetime). Your soul has a deep, ancient purpose just as the archetypes are timeless. We are ancient souls living in modern bodies. The core of who you are, the ethos of why you're here, the fabric of your existence, that's inside of you. So trust it. Move forward. And commit to your dharma, sun-being.

The Whole Crew Doin' Dharma

Imagine your dharma as the treasure, your life as the map, and each person you encounter as your guide. Some guides teach you what you want; others teach you what you don't; each reflects back a unique code that will bring you toward your dharma. As I was writing this book, I noticed I'd have exact conversations, receive random messages, and read quotes that sparked the insights I share in this book. Spirit worked through each of those people to plant the seeds of ideas for this book. **Every person you meet carries a code for you.**

Notice when you're deep in conversation, ideas flow through, but then when you're alone, your mind is in a loop? This is because as humans, we bounce off one another's feedback. When we are in deep conversation, we enter flow state through mutual energy exchange. To embody our dharma, we need the sounding board of others. Hearing about other people's experiences also gives us depth to better understand our own. Each person you meet gives you the opportunity to understand that archetype and better understand how the world works.

We all need support, and supporting others supports us. Support can come in many ways: from a friend, family member, community, mentor, teacher, etc. One of my favorite forms of support is called a Dharma Circle. I virtually meet with my Dharma Circle every two weeks to share what we are up to, what we are working on, and how we can support one another. It is like a mastermind experience except the focus is not on giving each other biz strategies, but rather supporting ourselves to continually find and redefine our truths and expressions. Having a Dharma Circle has been extremely beneficial to me when I've gone through pivotal turns in my dharma. Not only have I learned from the other women in the circle, but I've also been able to witness my own progress by sharing it with others.

HOW TO HOST A DHARMA CIRCLE

1. Come up with a list of several friends or post in a community that you'll be hosting a Dharma Circle. I recommend groups of around four so each person has about fifteen minutes to share and you can keep it to an hour. You can choose to all be in the same stage of finding your dharma or have a mix of stages for a range of perspectives. (We have a Dharma Support group in my membership community, called Rose Gold Goddesses, where you can find your crew!)

2. Begin with a meditation or prayer to set the intention. You can use mine below:

   Imagine living your dharma. You wake up each day knowing that today you are living life exactly as you were meant to. Each and every day you are tapping in to your unique gifts. You are healing the world just by emitting your vibration. You feel fulfilled, inspired, and deeply grateful. You are surrounded by an incredible community of like-minded people also living in alignment with their dharma. You are abundant and live the exact lifestyle you desire. You have full freedom to spend your time exactly as you want. You are touching so many people's lives. Feel the joy, the excitement, the gratitude, the honor. Put your hands on your heart and feel the joy of living in alignment with your dharma.

Once you feel ready, invite everyone to open their eyes.

3. Each person will take fifteen minutes to share what they're working through and what they can use support with, then open up the floor for the group to offer reflections, suggestions, and deeper questions to help them dive into their truth. Some days you may want to have a longer heart-share and other days you may just have a question you're working through and would like other people's perspectives. Keep a timer so each person does not go longer than fifteen minutes, to keep the energy moving. At the end ask "Do you feel complete?" to make sure everyone received what they needed.

4. Once each person has shared, everyone goes around again to repeat this affirmation: "I am so grateful to be [YOUR NAME] in this lifetime. I am so grateful to be living my dharma." Close the circle with a brief meditation and feel the frequency you've co-created! You are supported in living your dharma, sun-being!

Find Your Frentors

The best mentors I've had are frentors (friend mentors). Frentors are two individuals in a mutually beneficial friendship where both parties offer support and guidance to the other for their personal, spiritual, and professional growth. They may be friends you meet in a networking setting or friends with whom you have a previously existing relationship. They don't necessarily have to be on the same career path as you, but they can offer advice and perspective on your needs, and you can to them.

Not only do they offer me support and guidance, I offer it back to them. I learn so much from supporting my fellow frentors, and it teaches me so much about my own path. Our experiences often mirror each other, and I find just as much value in supporting them as I do when they support me. We bring out each other's sunshine! With frentorship, no one is on a pedestal, and you aren't afraid of getting real and vulnerable. I truly believe frentors are the mentors of a new paradigm.

Just as much as it's important to surround yourself with frentors, it's important to drop the frenemies. As you step into your dharma, you're going to trigger people who haven't stepped into theirs. Your light is going to shine too brightly for people who haven't met their own. Don't let that stop you from being the light that you are. You stepping into your light will in time inspire them to step into theirs. They're triggered by you because they see you've reclaimed a part of yourself they haven't had the courage to yet. It's not your job to get them to see the light that they are—it's your job to commit to the light that you are, which in turn reflects theirs.

HOW TO FIND YOUR FRENTORS

Join Rose Gold Goddesses. Imagine being supported by thousands of other goddesses committed to living their dharmas and blossoming into their highest selves with weekly workshops, deep-dive webinars, and resources by me. That's what being part of Rose Gold Goddesses is like! If you're looking for the highest-vibe spiritual sisterhood with our very own app, head over to rosegoldgoddesses.com! My 10-Day Discover Your Dharma course and meditations are awaiting you in there!

Attend workshops related to your interests and start conversations with the other people there. You already know you have one thing in common and, chances are, a lot more. Don't hold yourself back from reaching out; that would be withholding yourself from your dharmic code.

It goes down in the DM. Reach out to someone who inspires you on social media. It doesn't have to be a big influencer but anyone whose posts you resonate with. I've met most of my real-life best friends on Instagram, and I'm soul grateful I slid in their DMs.

Remember that cool person you met that you never ended up connecting with later? Send them a text. Invite them to an event or for a cup of coffee. It will not be weird even if it's a year later—they'll be flattered you thought of them!

Start a podcast. I've met so many of my friends through podcasting. It gives you a great excuse to have really deep conversations with people that you often wouldn't in your normal life. Podcasters often swap, so you'll both get to know tons of new people while sharing your message!

- **Give value back.** People like to spend time with someone they can learn from. What can you share with that person? Maybe you used to host events for a living or make graphics? Start with value and people naturally reciprocate. It is how we are wired.

The Universe Is Your #1 Fan

Above all, we are all always supported by the universe and can call upon it for energetic support. When I'm feeling overwhelmed, one of my favorite affirmations is: *"I receive the support that I need so that I can focus my energy on my dharma."* By declaring this, you open yourself up to receive the limitless support of the universe, whether it's through a person giving you a code or an idea planting in your crown chakra.

If you're at a place where you're confused, use the affirmation, *"Universe, make what is meant for me undeniable to me."* Whether it's making a decision or choosing the right person to hire, this states to the universe that you'd like clear guidance.

If you know what you need to do but it feels difficult, try the affirmation, *"May I walk to my dharma through kriya, flow, and ease."* This shifts the energy from trying to keep pace with life up to fully jogging with ease. The universe is listening. We just have to tell it what we want.

A QUICK RUNDOWN
FOR YOU SKIMMERS

If you're ready to vibe high with that dharma, you gotta put in the #werk, boo! Dharma doesn't like when you play hard to get. You gotta let it know you're ALL-IN. And that means not giving up when things get a little bit tough, because they will! That's actually when you gotta hold on tighter because once you move past those roadblocks, things get to a WHOLE OTHER level. When you feel like running away, giving up, or just ghosting on your dharma—remember why you're doing it. Get support from other people through a Dharma Circle and your frentors so you remember your why when all you're thinking is, "Why not give up?"

Being of Service

I have some news to share with you and I don't know how you're going to take it, but dharma is a service job. Now I know that doesn't sound sexy and suggests that I'm going to make you pass around flyers on the street, but hear me out. It's actually the sexiest part.

You see, when you're of service, you're tapped into that good shit. I'm talking about universal downloads, ultimate support, limitless inspiration, endless energy, radiant clarity, magnificent courage, never-ending wisdom bombs—all because you and the universe are on a team.

When you align your actions with the needs of the world, you are fueled with *prana*, the everlasting life force that circulates from the cosmos through your chakras down to Earth, and resurfaces again.

Being of service is the highest form of healing. It takes you out of your story and into higher existence—this is true wellness. Looking back on how I healed myself from my dire health problems, I now see that was through having a purpose greater than myself.

There are two types of people: the ones who are majorly turned on like, "Aww yeah, I work for Mother Earth!" and the others who are like, "Oh God, why'd I read this far!" But hear me out: **Service does not have to be a sacrifice.** In fact, service in alignment with your dharma is the ultimate win-win. You know when you helped a friend with a problem, and it gave you all this clarity and helped your own life? That's what this type of service is. **It's service through joy.**

When you follow your highest joy, you are naturally of service because you radiate that love to others. You make better decisions, create better solutions, and become part of moving the world forward. I used to think the only way I could help the world was to sacrifice my life. I thought I had to join the Peace Corps or Mother Teresa's mission to help others because those were the examples I saw. I even ended up going to George Washington University in pursuit of becoming an international human rights lawyer. However, I realized that it was not aligned with my truth and that I came to this Earth to serve and express in different ways.

I've realized that by creating the world I wish existed, I am changing the world. It started with a blog and it turned into a health-coaching career, which turned into books, which turned into online programs, which turned into speaking engagements, which turned into a podcast, which turned into a membership community, which turned into a movement of awakening people to radiate as their highest selves . . . and it's still expanding. I never set out to do any of this—I just kept following my joy and sharing it with others.

When you share what's moved you, you move others. It takes away the heavy responsibility of having to be the one superhero who's going to solve all the world's problems. Frankly, you cannot do this alone. And you weren't meant to. You were meant to shine so brightly in who you are that it inspires others to do the same. **Your job is not to sacrifice this lifetime to be of service, but to make your highest expression your form of service. When *you* change *your* world, you change the world.**

The new paradigm of service is through joy. When you choose joy, everything else is a ripple effect. Joy is available to us at any given moment, not just reserved for when we have it all figured out. Choosing joy is what helps you get there.

You cannot be of service if you do not celebrate yourself and your gifts. The era of undermining your magic has ended. By celebrating yourself, you inspire other people to celebrate themselves too. It's like a birthday party—fun for everyone involved.

We don't need any more martyrs. We don't need burned-out people so busy trying to save the world that they're suffering themselves. **The paradigm of the wounded healer has ended.** The new paradigm calls for empowered, aligned healers who are so fueled by life force they naturally want to expand it out to others. It's not just about their actions—just being around their energy is healing.

Your vibration is the ultimate act of service and the basis of your activism. When you are in alignment with your authentic code, you beam out positivity, and that shit is contagious. Your actions, your words, your energy, your compassion, your hug, your song, your dance is changing the world. Each of these micro expressions of yourself is your ultimate act of service. And best of all, it's effortless.

When you're truly embodying your dharma, you naturally move from a *"me* to *we"* mentality. It doesn't feel like a sacrifice to be of service, but the highest privilege. You realize that the more you give, the more *moksha,* liberation, you experience within. The greatest form of freedom is knowing you held nothing back in this lifetime.

Some of us are fueled by being of service to humanity, others to our community, still others to our family. Honor that. Trust that. That's your code. You are meant to be of service in the way you want to be. We need people in all areas.

Service in alignment with your dharma feels orgasmic. It's like when you're asked to help a friend about a subject you've been obsessed with and have so much to share. Service because you feel like you're "supposed to" does not.

Think about a village where everyone is of service in their own way; there are the medicine women, the mystics, the midwives, the priestesses, the warriors, the caretakers, the council leaders, and the artisans. We don't want the warriors taking care of our elderly or the mystics fighting our battles. We want everyone to be in their element. You are *part* of this village—you don't need to play all roles. Share your soul signature with the world and invite in others to share theirs with you too.

Doshas + Service

Each Dosha has its own way to be of service based on its natural-born energies. We were each designed with an array of all three Doshas but in varying amounts, so we can each be in service in unique ways. Because the needs of the universe are so diverse, our gifts are just as diverse. We need some people working directly with people, and others with media, and others with technology, and others with the law. We're all a tag team of Power Rangers, each with our own color, here to uplift humanity.

If we were trying to protect the oceans, the Vata could make visuals, the Pitta could organize a fundraiser, and the Kapha could facilitate a discussion. Teamwork makes the dream work, and we all have to focus on our zones of genius.

THE VATA WAY

The Vata way to be of service is through your ideas. Vata is air energy and thrives with the intangible: spirituality, creativity, arts, inventions. Vata's superpower is creativity. The question they must always ask themselves is, "How can I use my creativity to serve?" Some may feel like they're not actually being of service if they're not physically helping people, but that's untrue. We don't need everyone working at the homeless shelter. We need some people coming up with ideas to raise awareness about the homeless *issue*. The Vata way of helping is very big-picture, and Vata people tend to be drawn to larger-than-life causes like environmentalism or elevating global consciousness.

Vata energy brings a new wave to service. I recently went to a dance protest in which we danced throughout the streets of downtown LA in front of the major banks that are invested in the companies causing deforestation in the Amazon. Instead of being bored and angry, we wore face paint, samba danced, and brought out Amazonian elders to share their wisdom about honoring the Earth. That was a protest I would gladly be a part of every weekend.

Vata energy allows us to think outside the box. For example, Humans of New York is a social media account started by a photographer who would take quirky people's pictures on the city streets and ask them about their stories. That account alone has saved thousands of lives and raised awareness of causes that normally were swept under the rug. You don't have to give up what you're passionate about to be of service, but rather be of service through what you're passionate about.

THE PITTA WAY

The Pitta way of being of service is through leadership and execution. A Pitta is fire energy and wants to solve a specific problem in a tangible way. The Pitta does best when there's a clear goal at hand. For example, something like "saving the environment" will feel too intangible for them, and they won't have a way to measure their progress. They'd rather focus on one key goal, such as "reduce the district's plastic consumption by 50 percent." This makes them more likely to follow through because there are tangible action steps and a clear way to measure success. They're not going to back out of something once they've set a goal, whereas something as broad as "saving the environment" can easily be given up on because there's no way to measure the end result.

Pittas are all about sustainability and know that borrowing money and time from others isn't reliable long-term. They're not going door-to-door asking for donations; they're going to create their own business solutions. Pittas are very involved in social entrepreneurship, aligning social needs with a sustainable business. They are automation machines, and when they align this ability with service, the world benefits. The most aligned Pittas are the ones who have made their lives about being of service. They make money so that they can give back (while enjoying some in the process). It's not just about the paycheck; it's what that paycheck can do for the world.

THE KAPHA WAY

The Kapha way of being of service is through individual touch. Kapha is earth energy and exudes a loving, compassionate warmth that brightens up the days of those around them. They're the type of person who will volunteer at the school, shelter, or elder center, where everyone benefits from their warm and grounding energy. They are able to stay rooted even when people around them are experiencing pain, and they are profound space holders. Their patience allows them to remain consistent and present for people as they unfold. This is why they are coaches, nurses, teachers, caretakers, or parents. Without this contact, they feel meaningless.

Kapha energy allows us to humanize causes. They aren't concerned about the numbers; they're concerned about the people. They're the ones who will learn the individual stories of the people they're helping and make friends with the people they are being of service to. They excel at defusing difficult situations or helping someone through a breakthrough. In a world of anger, chaos, and hatred, the Kapha love is one of the things we need the most.

Which Dosha Are
You in Service To?

How do you prefer to work?

    A. On a team, managing people

    B. By myself, in my own element

    C. Directly in contact with other people

What do people compliment you most on?

    A. My ability to lead a team and bring projects to life

    B. My creative ideas and ability to see the big picture

    C. My patience and compassion

Someone comes to you needing help. How do you offer support?

    A. Listen to their problem for a bit, then come up with a strategy to solve it

    B. Tell them that their soul chose this for a reason and they have the strength within to overcome it

    C. Hold space for them to authentically express and ask questions to help them come up with their own answer

You're on a movie set. How do you want to get involved?

    A. Producer—analyze the budget to decide what scenes will be filmed, how, and with whom

B. Director/costume/hair/makeup—visualize the script and add artistic/dramatic aspects
C. Running lines with the actors—make sure everyone is feeling their best and putting in their full emotion

You want to end world hunger. How do you help?
A. Give a percentage of sales to an organization providing meals to the hungry
B. Create a riveting video about world hunger
C. Volunteer to cook meals at the local shelter

What excites you the most?
A. Building a business that transforms lives
B. Changing the way people think
C. Touching people's lives and hearts

A = PITTA
B = VATA
C = KAPHA

Any of the Doshas can really do any of these things, but they'll come at it from a different angle. A Vata coach will inspire you to connect with your higher self; a Pitta coach will motivate you to get into action; and a Kapha coach will remind you to love yourself. A coach can be all three things, but it's about the flavor that it gives you. Essentially what the Doshas do is give you full permission to be yourself.

Which Doshas do you relate to for being of service?

Dharma Brick Road

If you're freaking out about choosing the "wrong" path . . . don't worry. If there's one thing that I can leave you with at the end of this book, it's that all roads lead to your dharma—as long as you are in alignment with your truth. You cannot fuck this up as long as you're listening to yourself. Even if you take the wrong road momentarily, as soon as you tap back into truth you'll be redirected to the right one. The roads to your dharma intertwine and build upon each other. They're like a highway system that looks complex, but all roads lead to the same destination.

Getting onto the dharma brick road isn't always easy. People may tell you that you're batshit crazy. Why leave the well-lit, well-paved path everyone else is on for what appears to be a hodgepodge of roads, none of which have been driven on before? But that's when your inner GPS kicks in. The only difference is that it's our own voice instead of Siri, which makes us not "trust" it as much because we're so used to *others* choosing the way for us. **Imagine if you trusted your intuition as much as you trusted the opinions of others.**

So, how do you take that highway to your truth?

Truth is asking yourself the difficult questions . . . and being OK with not knowing the answers.

Truth is honoring your excitement as if it was a gem handed to you by the divine.

Truth is taking the treacherous, muddy path and paving it for the ones who will come next.

Truth is sticking to your vision even when it causes disapproval or anger in others.

Truth is realizing that the only commitment you have in this life-time is to be your truest self.

I don't think there's a single person in existence who's always, consistently lived their full truth. Truth is like a maze, and you know that you're going the wrong way only when you hit a dead end. Then there's always the opportunity to change directions. We are ever-changing beings. Everything in the universe is in motion: Our planet and our entire galaxy are revolving, expanding, and moving. Because we are a part of this galaxy, we too are constantly expanding and evolving. Even when it may appear we're standing still, we're moving forward, as long as we're committed to our truth.

When I was discovering my dharma, I first became aware of what I *didn't* want: someone else dictating my life, a meaningless job that I did just for money that didn't utilize the gifts that I knew I had. I could feel what I wanted more of: spirituality, writing, community, dance. I wasn't sure how it would all pan out, but I kept moving in the direction of what I wanted. Eventually, everything fell into place and is continuing to unfold, expand, and evolve. But I couldn't have seen it all from where I was. That's OK. Allow for room for the universe to surprise you. Spend less time stressing about what your dharma is and more time on the path toward what feels expansive at this moment.

I know the overwhelming feeling of wanting to do it all and not knowing where to start, but my best advice is: Bring one vision to life before bouncing to the next. Let your dharma be born, learn to walk, and live a little before ushering in the next one. That experience will prepare you to be the best dharma mama for what is to come.

The Evolvement of Your Dharma

Your dharma is your soul's expression—it is eternal and never-changing. However, its manifestations can vary greatly in your lifetime. Your dharma is like your mission statement on a website—however the services, About page, photos, and branding will shift as you develop. For example, let's say your dharma is to bring beauty to this world. You may do so as a child by drawing, then later through working on hair and nails, then later through interior design, then later still through graphic design and painting. The dharma is the same but its expressions are varied.

My dharma is to raise consciousness and empower others to blossom into their highest selves, and its expressions vary through time. I can do this by writing books, recording podcasts, hosting events, building community, creating social media content, teaching healing and embodiment through dance, and so much more. Though the expressions are different, the dharma is the same.

Your dharma is the red thread that has been carried across all stages of your life that have brought you to your powers. Your dharma may be healing the wounded feminine by being a therapist, then later working with the moon cycles, then later doing relationship coaching. Your dharma may be to bring healing sounds to this planet through playing instruments, producing music, singing, and songwriting. Your dharma may be to nurture others so they can be seen and loved through teaching, parenting, and caregiving. The dharma is eternal; its expression is fluid.

The Doshas inform us of the red thread across the dharma.

Those with more Vata energy tend to have multiple projects running at once because their energy is so dynamic. They become bored doing just one thing day in and day out, and prefer the freedom of constant evolvement. They wear many different hats, are involved with different projects at the same time, and go through many drastic changes throughout their lives, which is simply part of their dharma. Their dharmic work is to bring the high visions they carry into the world so they can be shared and experienced by others.

Those with more Pitta energy prefer to concentrate on one thing at a time and give it all of their energy. They're determined, driven, and know that their focus won't be clear if they're simultaneously fulfilling another career. They always have other business ideas in the back of their minds, but don't fully dive in until their main venture is in a good enough place for others to support the vision.

Those with more Kapha energy gravitate toward having one or two major roles throughout their lives. They prefer to stick with something they love and go really deep with it, especially when it uses their natural nurturer abilities. Their dharma is focused on their interpersonal relationships. They're less likely to define themselves by what they do and more by the lives they touch. Parenthood often plays a large role in their dharma, and they often find their life's work through this experience.

Different Dharma Archetypes may be heightened at different points of our lives. For example, many of us were more connected to our Activist archetype in our younger years, but the bureaucracy in politics kept us from continuing down that path. We disassociate from that side of ourselves, and other archetypes take stronger hold. However, if we're being completely true to ourselves, we know that the Activist still lives within us, just expressed in different ways—perhaps you use social media to share important messages or get involved with your local government.

When you start fully living your dharma, you'll reunite with the missing parts of you that you let go of in order to fit in, realizing that you were meant to stand out. You finally become the person you've been too busy, too afraid, too intimidated to be. The very aspects of you that didn't "make sense" and got crowded out will take center stage. You'll remember the passion you once had for saving the animals, or the hours you used to spend reading magical novels, or how much you loved gathering in community, and bring it back into your life with higher wisdom.

Discovering your dharma doesn't mean you'll stop changing once you've discovered it. It just means that you are finally operating at the full expression of who you are, and that you have paved that path to let all parts of you know that it is safe to be seen and show up in the way that you were meant to. Living in alignment with your dharma is a frequency—it is expressing completely who you are at this moment and also remaining open to the evolution of who you will become.

A QUICK RUNDOWN
FOR YOU SKIMMERS

Dharma is a service job, and it's one you're super stoked about having. Because true service is not a sacrifice; it's your greatest form of joy. The world doesn't need any more wounded healers. We need lit-up, ecstatic sun-beings so enthusiastic about what they do that they naturally want to beam their expression to others. When you truly tap into this essence, you can't help but share your radiant self with the world—it's too much light to be contained!

The Vata way of service is to make it innovative; the Pitta way is to get #results; the Kapha way is through adding faces to those we're advocating for. When you follow the dharma brick road, all will come full circle. You'll see the red thread that's been carrying you across all the stages of your life and how it's been perfectly guiding you toward your dharma. You'll realize you needed the experiences you've had to truly embody the sun-being you were born to be.

All Roads Lead to Dharma

I f you're reading this book and are still confused as to what your dharma is, let me lay it out for you. The truth is, we all have one shared dharma. Every single one of us came to Earth for the exact same reason. Yes, we have different gifts and strengths and ways to express it, but the reason is universal. Ready for it? Your dharma. My dharma. Our dharma. Is to help others embody their dharmas.

That's it. We all came to this planet to activate one another in our own unique ways. If you can help someone else gain clarity, find courage, and take aligned action in pursuit of their dharma, you're fuckin' doing it. It's just not as complicated as we think it is. It's the domino effect I told you about at the beginning: We're all interconnected by a cosmic web of energy, and we can only move as forward as the world does. Life is like a potluck; it's only as good as the food and energy everyone brings to it. So make this world a little more flavorful by doing your dharma.

Dharma is not just a theory—it's something to be experienced. **Inspiration is an invitation by your dharma.** Excitement is your soul's language, saying, "Pay attention here, I have something for you." Now it's your job to step into that and explore what is awaiting you on the other side.

Your dharma is knocking on your door, waiting for you to invite it in. Imagine you're reaching up, grabbing a piece of the cosmos and pulling it down to Earth. You're ushering something to life that has never existed before, bridging two dimensions. You are transmuting the intangible to the tangible, so it can be shared with others. Now all you have to do is take aligned action.

This is the part where a lot of people get stuck, especially in the spiritual community. They see the clear vision of how to end world hunger in their meditation, then just continue drinking their smoothie, hoping Elon Musk will solve it. The idea came to you because you were meant to birth it. You are the perfect vessel to bring it to life. All you have to do is trust yourself.

The idea is gifted to you, but the steps are for you to figure out. That figuring out is your training; you don't want to skip that part. **The only path to clarity is through action**. You don't have to know every step you're going to take in order to start. As you take steps forward, the path continues to show up. Just begin dancing and the choreography will come.

Think of your dharma like a mountain range. In order to get to the first peak, you need to begin your hike. Through hiking, you become stronger, learn how to use your energy, better understand the terrain. Even when you reach that first summit, you see there are many more waiting for you to explore. **Dharma is not about the destination, but rather the journey of embodying who you truly are at any given moment.**

All big dharmas start simply. We often look at the enormity of our dharmas and remain at a standstill because we don't know where to start. That first step can be a meditation, a conversation, a thought, an email, an audition, a curiosity. Then let the next step unfold. Excitement will always light the path, even as you're quivering with the next move forward.

Your only purpose is to ground ideas from the cosmos to Earth through your chakras. You are here as a conduit. Anytime you're stuck, just notice what chakra you are stuck on and bring it back into balance.

- If your root chakra is blocked and you don't feel grounded, reconnect with your vessel. Spend time in nature, preferably with bare feet so you can receive the negative ions of the Earth. Turn your phone off to get out of your head and into your body. Use the Dharma Embodiment Practice in Chapter 8.
  Repeat the affirmation, "It's safe for me to live my dharma."

- If your sacral chakra is blocked and you aren't feeling joy, cultivate pleasure. Feel pleasure in all things, from the sun hitting your skin to eating a delicious chocolate to sacred intimacy. Move that pleasure through your body and allow yourself to truly receive. Know that you deserve to feel bliss. Belly dance, Tantra, and Taoist practices are extremely healing for the sacral.
  Repeat the affirmation, "My dharma brings me the greatest pleasure."

- If your solar plexus is blocked and you're having a little identity crisis, practice saying "yes" and "no." Say yes to the opportunities that expand you, even if they scare you. Say no to the ones that make you feel contracted, but also "make sense." Set boundaries for yourself so that you can have others stick to them too. PS: You can say no without having to explain yourself.

Repeat the affirmation, "My yesses and noes are sacred."

- If your heart chakra is blocked and you aren't feeling connected to your dharma, be near animals and loved ones. Feel the vibration of love in your heart. Eye-gazing, touch, and human connection are extremely potent for opening up the heart chakra, as are heart-openers (backbends).
  Repeat the affirmation, "My dharma is to embody love."

- If your throat chakra is blocked and you have a hard time putting your thoughts into words, begin writing, even if it's messy. Let yourself write without editing. Slowly the truth will find itself in your words.
  Repeat the affirmation, "I am a creative channel for my dharma."

- If your third eye is blocked and you aren't able to think clearly, visualize. Imagine you as your highest self; the radiance in your eyes; the glow of your skin; the confidence you exude. Ask, "What would my highest self do right now?" and allow yourself to receive.
  Repeat the affirmation, "I see my dharma clearly through my third eye."

- If your crown chakra is blocked and you're feeling disconnected from your connection to the universe, meditate.
  Create space. Breathe. Allow for the sacred pause. No need for words here.

I'm rooting for you. We're all rooting for you. We need you, sun-being.

It's *Just* Your Dharma

I want to close this book by reminding you that even though discovering your dharma feels like the most important thing in your life and totally overwhelming, you don't have to take it so seriously. Freaking out over it is just going to push it away and cause you to jump into something that isn't your dharma.

Yes, your dharma is the most important thing you can do in this lifetime, but it's just *this* lifetime. Your soul has been here many times before and will continue across planes, dimensions, and galaxies, coming back again and again until you embody your dharma. So if you don't get it in this lifetime, don't sweat it. You'll be back. But let's aim for this one.

The first step is knowing that it's there. You see it from the corner of your eye and know it's coming for you. Now turn the focus inward. Turn up your highest self and show up as her so you two can meet. You must allow the energy of ease, play, and fluidity into your life in order to let the dharma find you. And this means truly embodying it, not pretending you're having "fun" while you're side-eyeing your dharma like a stalker.

The energy of *tension* is never one of *manifestation* and *creation*. Tension is just going to prevent you from seeing what is so obvious. Ease will allow you to open up to your dharma, which is right under your third eye. The ego rushes; the highest self is patient.

The best thing you can do with all of this knowledge is to let it simmer. Really land on the concepts of this book and go back to the ones that spoke to you, or that you're unsure of. Your subconscious is doing the work, so allow it space to unravel and unfold. From this state of higher awareness, observe the signs. They've been there all along, and now you're more attuned to their subtle vibration. Notice the synchronicities in the coming weeks: what sentence pops up, what podcast episode starts playing, what opportunities present themselves, what you feel yourself getting excited about. **All it takes is one shift in consciousness to let the entire path illuminate itself.** You may meet a person, or go to a place, or read something that changes your entire existence. Trust it. Let yourself follow the path your dharma is paving for you, with seeds of excitement planted along the way. The more you surrender to the flow, the more you'll grow. Move toward what feels expansive.

Note that I said "expansive," not "good"—the two are not always synonymous. For example, the predominant emotion when you leave a job you despise might be nerves and terror, but it will definitely make you feel expansive. Moving to a new city may feel contractive at first, but then lead to further expansion. Saying no to your family's expectations may feel shameful at first, but will definitely help you expand.

What does expansive feel like for you? For me, it feels like stretching out in nature knowing I have all the space and freedom in the world. It feels like putting myself out there in an uncomfortable way because it expands my vision of what's possible for myself and others. Expansive feels like saying yes to a project I get butterflies thinking about and ushering it to life. It feels like saying no to a request that's not in alignment with my soul mission at this time. It feels like sharing my dance, even when I feel self-conscious. It feels like expanding the norms of what has ever been possible for me and my ancestors.

What does expansive feel like for you, physically, mentally, and emotionally? When have you felt expansive?

What does contractive feel like for you? For me, it feels like sitting in an airplane seat for far too long, hungry to stretch out my legs and breathe. It feels like repeating myself, over and over, rather than letting the new thoughts in my mind come through. It feels like being stuck in a conversation about the news and weather with people unwilling to go deeper. Contractive felt like when I'd try to convince myself that I didn't need to do what I loved professionally but could just keep it as a hobby. Contractive feels like lying to yourself. It feels like taking a step backward away from what you know is best for your soul. But the good thing is, you can always choose to expand again and use that lesson to propel you forward. **Expansion is your divine nature.**

Contractive	Expansive
Even though this is difficult, I have to stick it out because that's just what you do.	Even though this is difficult, it's bringing me to my higher truth.
I don't really have a direction but I'm just taking the steps I'm "supposed" to.	I'm not sure of all the steps, but I know I'm moving in the right direction.
Why is this happening to me?	What is this teaching me?
I doubt this is related to my dharma.	I trust that I am in alignment with my dharma.

When you're expanding, you can feel like you're jumping off a building, unsure if your wings will actually unfold. You've seen other people do it, but part of you still doubts that you too can fly. This disbelief is exactly *what* keeps your wings from expanding. It's like saying, "Show me proof of spirituality and then I'll believe it." You have to believe it to feel the proof. You can't say, "I'll expand if you can guarantee this certain outcome." Our own constrictive thinking is what keeps us from that expansion. The proof, the plan, the play-by-play just don't exist. There are infinite paths that you can take, and each will unlock different things at different times.

There is no one-size-fits-all approach to dharma. Yes, everything happens for a reason, but also *you are that reason*. We are walking the fine line between destiny and free will, and while there is a grand plan for us, we may not get to the treasure chest in this lifetime if we don't make it a priority. You are a sovereign being with a free mind, and honestly, you don't have to live up to your dharma if you don't want to. I doubt you're that person if you're reading this book, but you may have a family member or friend who's like that, and it may pain you to see it. You need to remember that it's their journey. The best thing that you can do is embody your dharma and lead by example.

No matter what shape your dharma takes, underlying it is this: Your dharma is to be a light in this world. You were meant to shine so brightly that you make the world a more illuminated place. The world doesn't need your perfection—it needs your fullest expression. **Today is the best time in history to live your dharma because of the global awakening that is happening.** There is so much support waiting for you to say yes, and so many causes waiting for your support. We are living in a time of utmost duality, the highest of highs and the lowest of lows. Simply put, this is exactly why our souls *have* come through. We are part of the cleanup crew here to undo this mess and uplift humanity. The world has gotten to a place where we are hurting each other and the planet without seeing that we are all connected. We are here to restore the equilibrium.

More and more old souls are returning with experience and courage to face these issues with strength and wisdom. People are awakening, questioning their lifelong beliefs, and recognizing that they have an important role to play in healing humanity. It is never too late or too soon. **Your realization is an invitation to take action now.** Your desire to serve is the only prerequisite needed. We are remembering the ancient ways to heal our bodies, awaken our minds, and connect to our spirits because these tools are more needed today than ever before. It's time for us to come together, across generational lines, and share our magic to elevate the vibration of the planet.

We are more than human beings. **We are sun-beings, here to embody the energy of the vibrant sun.** When we live our dharmas, we invite the rest of the world to activate the radiant power within themselves, too. The more we shine our light, the more its luminosity spreads. When others feel our uplifting rays, they ignite the sun within them, too, and we join hands in the sky as stars. It's time we turn our light all the way up, for the planets in the back who haven't yet remembered their radiance.

The Earth is our body, the water our blood, the air our breath, the fire our passion, the ether our spirit. Together, we collectively create the five elements, the three Doshas, and the nine archetypes, each with our own unique Dharma Blueprint to raise consciousness.

This is a call to all Vatas, Pittas, Kaphas, Teachers, Nurturers, Visionaries, Entrepreneurs, Artists, Activists, Entertainers, Researchers, Warriors, and every type of sun-being to rise up, share your gifts, and shine your light. The world can only come into balance when we all show up as our fullest, most expressed selves. And best of all—it can be a lot of fun.

Truthfully, your dharma and mine are the same: to raise consciousness and help others discover their dharmas, too. So now that you remember yours, *let's awaken the world together.*

ACKNOWLEDGMENTS

I would first like to thank universal Source wisdom for channeling through me to usher these words out into the world. Thank you for choosing me as your vessel.

Thank you to the twenty-three-year-old girl in me who did not give up, for being courageous in a time when it mattered most. I'm here because you persevered.

Thank you to each person living their dharma I met in those transformative years in Bali and India. You showed me it was possible to live mine. Thank you to my Shamanic teacher Malaika for reminding me that this journey was mine to live, fully, freely, and unapologetically.

Thank you to my parents for giving me this opportunity of life, for setting up both the transformative opportunities and the obstacles that have allowed me to embody my dharma. If it weren't for your support, and even disapproval, I wouldn't be here.

Thank you to my husband for leading by example, being as committed to his dharma as I am to mine, and constantly encouraging me to dream bigger.

Thank you to Deepak Chopra for believing in me, before my first book was even out, and for being a lifelong role model.

Thank you to my executive editor, Cara, and the Chronicle Prism team for believing in the concept of this book, to Jen for editing down my many words, and to Brandi and the UTA team for supporting my vision.

To all seen and unseen beings who have supported me in this process, I am of utmost gratitude.

Atma Namaste.

ABOUT THE AUTHOR

Sahara Rose is an ancient soul in a modern body, here on a mission to awaken people into their fullest expressions so they can blossom into their highest selves. She has been called "a leading voice for the millennial generation into the new paradigm shift" by Deepak Chopra. She is a three-time bestselling author, host of the top-ranked *Highest Self Podcast*, keynote speaker, and founder of Rose Gold Goddesses. She has been featured on the cover of *Yoga Journal* as well as in *Vogue* and *Forbes* and on NBC, and has spoken at Google, Facebook, and Harvard. When she's not writing books or creating content, you can find her dancing, DJing, and drumming.